Published by the
American Sailing Association
and International Marine
10 9 8 7 6 5 4 3 2

Questions regarding the contents of
this book should be addressed to:
American Sailing Association
13922 Marquesas Way
Marina del Rey, CA 90292
(310) 822-7171 Phone
(310) 822-4741 Fax

Questions regarding trade
distribution of this book should be
addressed to International
Marine/TAB Books; Division of
McGraw-Hill, Inc.;
Blue Ridge Summit, PA 17294

CRUISING
FUNDAMENTALS

By

Harry Munns

Edited by

Hal Sutphen

Illustrations/Design

Vince Mattera

International Marine Publishing Camden, Maine

Table of Contents

Section I
Getting Acquainted

Section II
Getting Familiar

Section III
The Voyage

Section IV
Arrival & Living Aboard

Section V
Problem Solving/Trouble Shooting

Appendices

THE ASA
AND SAILING EDUCATION

The American Sailing Association works through sailors, sailing instructors, sailing schools and charter fleets nationwide. Our purpose is to bring organization and professional standards to sailing education. Boating safety through education has been our goal since we were founded over a decade ago.

The ASA Sailing Log Book contains the comprehensive sailing standards which represent the heart of the ASA system. These performance objectives give sailors a set of goals and a means by which to gauge their own knowledge and abilities. Certified, professional sailing instructors administer the standards at ASA sailing schools nationwide. Through certification to these standards the ASA provides the individual with a reliable way to document achievement in sailing.

The ASA Log Book contains a detailed list of requirements for each standard, space to affix certification seals and a record of sailing experience. Sailors use the Log Book as their personal passport and sailing auto-biography. Charter companies and rental operations worldwide recognize the quality of the ASA standards and accept the ASA Log Book as proof of knowledge and experience.

ASA sailing schools get thousands of new sailors started each year. Increasing numbers of experienced sailors have begun to "challenge" the ASA standards. They are tested on their knowledge and ability without the necessity of attending classes. ASA certifications are then awarded for the appropriate certification levels.

The ASA has made a positive difference in the quality of American sailing education. With the continued support of professional sailing schools and instructors our work will continue and expand. We commend the growing number of people who improve their knowledge and enjoyment of sailing through the ASA system and its various elements, including Cruising Fundamentals.

ABOUT CRUISING FUNDAMENTALS

Cruising Fundamentals was written to help developing sailors make the transition from daysailing and basic cruising to intermediate coastal cruising. Any sailor whose goal is to cruise 30 to 50 foot boats in coastal waters will find a wealth of practical information within its covers.

The material covered in this text corresponds to the Bareboat Chartering Standard in the ASA Log Book. Basic Keelboat Sailing and Basic Coastal Cruising precede Bareboat Chartering in the ASA system. Many topics applicable to the previous two certification levels are absent from Cruising Fundamentals. These "basic" subjects are addressed in the ASA text Sailing Fundamentals.

A comprehensive, working knowledge of the material in this book will prepare an individual for ASA certification. Whatever your goal - from confident boat ownership to distant bareboat chartering - this book will help provide the necessary tools.

The book is divided into five sections. Sections I through IV are divided into two sub-sections, Sailing Knowledge and Sailing Skills. Sailing Knowledge addresses the sailing subjects which are theoretical in nature. Sailing Skills are the elements of sailing which must be performed and practiced.

Read the book and learn the lessons which it has to teach; but remember that learning to sail is learning to perform a task. Any book, including this one, is nothing more than a written invitation to sail. A world filled with tradition, beauty, excitement and relaxation awaits just beyond the dock, so stow Cruising Fundamentals somewhere dry when you're finished reading and get out and do some sailing!

Acknowledgements

This book was developed from the knowledge and wisdom of teachers, students, sailors and authors; too numerous to name.

Great thanks go to Hal Sutphen, whose fathomless knowledge is only exceeded by a willingness to roll up his sleeves and get the job done.

Cindy Wise, Anthony Sandberg, Dan Glennon and Rich Jepsen provided invaluable help developing the manuscript.

Vince Mattera brilliantly created a book from what had been merely a collection of words.

Thanks also to Lenny Shabes for his fine photographic work.

The American Sailing Association and International Marine Publishing have my sincerest gratitude for the opportunity to make my tiny contribution to the world of sailing, a world that continues to thrill, fascinate and satisfy me.

Cover Photo:
Clint Clement
Courtesy of *The Moorings*
"The Best Sailing
Vacations In The World"

Photographic models:
Sherri Corr, Steve Dahlberg, Peter DeWolf, Karen Hennessey,
Lorrie Hill, Kathy Kachurka, Bob Lane, Don Mattera, Chris Manning, Beth Pincince

SECTION I

Sailing Knowledge

GETTING ACQUAINTED

"I wish I had a stone for the knife," the old man said after he had checked the lashing on the oar butt. "I should have brought a stone." You should have brought many things, he thought. But you did not bring them old man. Now is no time to think of what you do not have. Think of what you can do with what there is.

The Old Man and the Sea
-Ernest Hemingway

More recently a pragmatic sailor said that ,"There are no department stores or gas stations at sea." In other words, your boat and its contents must provide for your needs from the time it leaves the dock until it returns or arrives at another destination.

Proper preparation and education can instill the knowledge and confidence necessary to handle most situations which are likely to arise on a sailboat. This theme summarizes one of *Cruising Fundamentals* ' basic lessons and it reappears throughout the book. Section I introduces you to some unfamiliar aspects of sailing a 30 to 50 foot cruising sailboat in coastal waters. Familiarity with the boat and its equipment is absolutely essential to safe sailing. "How much could there possibly be to learn about a 30 to 50 foot boat?" you might ask. The answer follows.

TOPSIDE ORIENTATION

Stepping aboard a larger cruising boat you will notice instantly that there are a number of differences between it and the more familiar small sailboat. The feel of the boat under your weight and movement is more stable due to additional length, beam and ballast. However, that stability disappears almost entirely when the boat sails in turbulent waters. Add steep waves and a churning sea and the boat feels more like a dinghy than the ship it resembles at the dock.

International America's Cup Class yachts sail on San Diego Bay.

MAST HEIGHT

Mast height also increases to accommodate additional sail area. The manufacturer's specifications, which are usually stowed below, should list mast height. That measurement usually indicates height from the waterline, not from the deck. Mast height is around one and one half times boat length on most standard cruising boats. Even International America's Cup Class Yachts, which push every possible tolerance in pursuit of speed, have masts in this range.

You need to know the mast measurement to navigate through bridges and under power lines. Some bridges will have the vertical clearance posted on a piling or abutment. Charts are a more reliable way of planning a route. One unexpected, low bridge can force you to backtrack many miles down a canal or river. Worse yet, mis-calculation could bring the rig down. Either consequence results in a bad day. Coast Pilots and harbor charts list the vertical clearance below bridges and power lines. Study both carefully before passing below any obstruction. (more on Coast Pilots and charts later in Section IV)

SAIL PLAN

The formula linking the boat's dimensions and the sail area is one of the most challenging aspects of yacht design. The amount of square footage must be appropriate for the shape and weight of the hull and keel. Too much keel weight and the boat sails slowly in all but gale force winds. Too much sail area will cause excess heeling, instability and excess weather helm. A well designed sailboat must have enough sail area to sail well in light winds. When wind increases there must be ways to gradually reduce sail area. This will ease weather helm and reduce strain on the mast and rigging.

Staysail placement on a cutter rig

THE SLOOP

Many designers choose a sloop rig: one mast which will accommodate two sails, the mainsail and the jib. Most racing and coastal cruising yachts manufactured today are sloop rigged. Sail area can be reduced by taking multiple reefs in the main and changing to smaller jibs.

THE CUTTER

Some single masted boats place the mast farther aft than a sloop to include a staysail in their sail plan. This makes the rig a Cutter and it is typically 35 feet or longer. The jib-like staysail occupies part of the foretriangle, the area bordered by the forward edge of the mast, the forestay and the foredeck.

Some staysails have their own boom which makes them "Club Footed" staysails. Staysails usually accompany jibs measuring less than 150% of the foretriangle.

The addition of a staysail provides a cutter with equal or greater sail area forward, compared to a sloop, while increasing sail choice options in a freshening breeze. Sailors often choose to drop the jib altogether as the wind increases. The staysail tacks inside the foretriangle and is sheeted inside the shrouds. The chance of fouling jib sheets and wear and tear on the crew are minimized when the staysail works without a jib. On a beat a club-footed staysail, which uses a single sheet, will usually be made fast because trim is the same on both tacks. The staysail, therefore, becomes self-tacking.

SPLIT RIGS

Most modern day spars are alloy extrusions. Taller masts require greater girth and thicker walls. Weight aloft increases which, any yacht designer will tell you , is not where you want to concentrate the weight on a sailboat.

Place another mast on deck and the height of the first, main mast, can be reduced. The weight of the spars and sails is brought closer to deck by spreading the necessary sail area over a greater distance fore and aft. The area of the sails will also be reduced making them lighter and more manageable. The advantages of an additional spar and rigging do, however, come with a price. The boat's overall wind resistance increases which effects speed and stability.

Boats with two masts are commonly called split rigs. Two types are most often seen among today's cruising yachts. Each places the taller, main mast, forward of the shorter mizzen mast. A Ketch has a somewhat larger mizzen sail and the mizzen mast stands forword of the rudder post. Yawls have comparatively smaller mizzen sails and their mizzen masts are positioned aft of the rudder post.

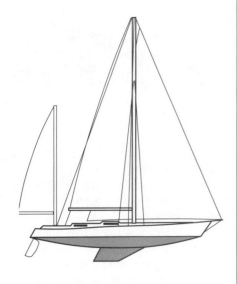

The yawl (top) has become much less common than the ketch (below) in modern yacht design.

HYDRAULICS

Some cruising boats, like their smaller cousins, require backstay tension to bend the mast, tighten the forestay and flatten the mainsail. Smaller boats usually accomplish the task with a split backstay and a tensioning device which uses a tackle to draw the sides of the backstay together.

The rigs on some larger boats have been designed for stability and sail trim without backstay adjustments. Others will use the mechanical tackle system. Another option which has become popular in recent years is the use of hydraulic backstay adjusters. They employ a cylinder, which usually attaches directly to the backstay, and a pump, which may be attached directly to the backstay or located elsewhere in the cockpit.

A valve allows you to pump hydraulic fluid into the cylinder, causing backstay tension to increase, or it releases fluid from the system to reduce backstay pressure. Generally, the valve directs the pump's pressure into the system when the knob is turned clockwise. Pressure escapes when the knob is turned counter clockwise. You may find it easy to remember that pressure flows out when turned counterclockwise, just like water flowing out of a faucet.

Most boats equipped with hydraulic backstays will have some sort of calibration system. Look for a pressure gauge or a ruler on the backstay. Specifications for adjusting hydraulics come from either the manufacturer or the company which built the spars. Backstay pressure should be left off. Motoring into waves may require a slight pressure increase to keep the rig from pumping.

Backstay tension will most frequently be required while sailing to weather. As the wind increases, backstay tension must also increase to tighten the forestay and keep the mainsail flat. Familiarize yourself with tension recommendations and avoid excess backstay pressure. It could cause rig failure.

HYDRAULIC BOOM VANG

Everything which requires power demands more power on a bigger boat. Boom vang adjustments on smaller sail boats were accomplished with a manageable block and tackle system. That method becomes impractical on a mainsail which has double or triple the size and force. A hydraulic boom vang increases pulling power and reduces crew strain. A hydraulic vang operates like a hydraulic backstay. Some units use the same valve and pump by adding a switch which directs their forces to either backstay or vang. Mechanical adjustments become more difficult when they approach overload. Hydraulics may apply more force than is necessary or safe without ever becoming difficult to operate. Become familiar with operating manuals and get a briefing from an experienced individual to avoid a world of problems.

Hydraulic fluid enters and escapes from the hydraulic backstay cylinder through the attached flexible hose.

RUNNING RIGGING

Adapting from one boat to another or one size boat to another becomes easier when sailors learn to recognize the function of equipment rather than its form. Halyards, for example, might run inside the mast on one boat and outside on the next. Main sheets could easily be led and secured six different ways on six different boats. Yet the function of a halyard is always the same, as is the function of a main sheet. A wise sailor understands the task he or she wishes to perform, then identifies the machinery which performs that task.

One of the most time saving innovations in modern sailboat cruising was the advent of rollerfurling jibs. The entire jib is rolled up onto the forestay by means of a furling system. A quick look at the forestay will indicate whether a boat is equipped with roller furling. For the moment, identify the furled jib with sheets attached, the furling drum at the base of the forestay and the furling line leading back to the cockpit. We explore roller furler operation in the Sailing Skills portion of this section.

Halyards

Function and form come into play when searching for halyards on a new boat. Larger sailboats are apt to have more halyards than smaller boats. More than one developing sailor has thrown his or her hands up in frustration, unable to locate the halyard on a new boat because it was not located in the old, familiar place.

Remember that the main halyard always exits the aft part of the masthead and it will be as easy to locate as the ice box. Normally, three cables lead aft from the masthead; the backstay, topping lift and main halyard. The backstay can be quickly identified as the one which leads furthest aft. The topping lift runs to the aft end of the boom. Follow the remaining cable and it will lead to the end of your main halyard.

Next, locate all of the halyards as they descend the mast. Internal halyards will exit somewhere within reach of a person standing at the base of the mast. External halyards will be visible the entire height of the mast. You should be able to create some slack by sweating

Running rigging is led over the cabin top to the mast.

(pulling the exposed section of the halyard away from the mast). Some vigorous tugs on each halyard should eventually create movement on the end of the one you just identified as the main.

Sometimes a main halyard will lead to the end of the boom, just like the topping lift. The topping lift probably leads around a block and inside the boom while the halyard terminates with a shackle. If there are two shackles, then the topping lift operates like a halyard, running over a sheave at the top of the mast and securing somewhere on the mast. The halyard will lead to a winch and a heavier cleat. The topping lift requires less purchase and probably just ties off to a small cleat.

Occasionally cruising sailboats employ halyards made entirely of braided line. These are rare and, other than a tendency to stretch, present no new problems.

When halyards arrive at the base of the mast they require a winch and a cleat. Winches are most commonly located on the mast, on the deck near the mast or on the cabin top near the cockpit. The following items may be used together or separately to guide and secure halyards.

- Blocks
- Cheek blocks
- Turning blocks
- Jam cleats
- Sheet stoppers
- Pad eyes

SHEETS

Jib sheets attach to the clew the same way they do on smaller boats. Roller furling jibs must have their sheets attached and cleated when they are furled to keep the sail from unrolling. Follow jib sheets aft from the bow to determine how they lead through the fairlead blocks to the winches. Turning blocks are often used to alter the angle at which the sheets meet the winches. Jib sheets on boats without roller furling attach and are led the same way they are on smaller boats with the possible exception of passing through turning blocks.

Main sheets come in all different shapes and forms. Remember the function and the form will be easier to discover. Boats 30 feet and larger always have a winch to make mainsail trim easier.

Hydraulic boom vangs have already been discussed but the familiar mechanical vang is not uncommon on larger boats. The vang may have more purchase (additional blocks) and might lead to the cockpit. Once again, remember the function and find the form.

The Cunningham looks like a vang block and tackle except with smaller gear and lighter line. It can be found around the gooseneck area and will attach to a grommet a few inches up the luff from the tack. It applies additional tension to the luff to improve sail trim upwind in a freshening breeze.

The outhaul works the same way it did in a small boat except that very large boats may use a small boom-mounted winch for adjustments.

A roller furling jib partly unfurled

(A) Lifelines, (B) Bow Pulpit, (C) Toe Rail

BOW AREA

Lifelines run forward and aft along the edge of the deck. They are held in place by stanchions with one line running along the top of each stanchion and one running through the middle. Some smaller sailboats feature lifelines but virtually every cruising sailboat comes equipped with these safety devices. They may save you in an emergency but never intentionally bet your life on a lifeline. They may fail when they are needed most. Never stand or sit on lifelines.

The lifelines attach to the bow pulpit, a rigid framework of plated tubing. It provides a loose cage which keeps people and equipment from slipping off the bow. Crew members on the dock also find it helpful for manually maneuvering the bow. Halyards may rest on the bow pulpit when not in use and running lights may also be mounted on it. Sailors who use the bow pulpit to soften the impact of a hard landing are usually surprised by the size of the repair bill.

The toe rail runs below the lifelines along the entire perimeter of the deck. It forms a rigid, metal wall rising a few inches above the deck with holes through it every few inches. The toe rail makes a wonderful place to attach lines. It also serves as an emergency foot hold when traveling along a heeling deck.

Fairleads or chocks guide dock and towing lines overboard from deck cleats. Tide, current, wind and waves cause a boat to move continuously while tied to a dock or while being towed. The moving bulk of the boat grinds the dock lines against the points where they contact the boat. Fairleads provide a smooth surface which minimizes wear, known as chafing. Lines are often coated with rubber, plastic or leather to further reduce chafe in the areas where they pass through the fairleads.

The forestay attaches to the hull by means of a stem fitting. It performs the same function as it would on a smaller boat except it often has a bow roller molded into it. The bow roller acts as a fairlead for the anchor rode when the anchor is lowered or raised. Some bow rollers are designed to store an anchor between the metal plates on either side of the roller. A pin passes through a hole in each plate. In the case of a plow or CQR anchor, a small eye is molded into the anchor's crown. With the anchor placed between the two plates the pin passes through the eye and is secured on the outside of both plates. The anchor sits immovably until the time comes to deploy it.

Anchors may also be kept in an anchor locker whose doors are molded into the deck at the bow. Unlatching and lifting the doors exposes anchor and rode. Anchor rode for bow mounted anchors is usually stowed in a chain locker below deck. The rode passes through a chain pipe when it travels between the deck and the locker.

Heavier ground tackle creates more work. A hand operated anchor winch or an electric windlass can make life at the bow a lot easier. The vast number of types and models would make any worthwhile treatment of the subject impossible in this text. Specific instructions are available from manuals, instructors and charter agents.

Somewhere along the deck's edge you will notice round, slightly raised disks about four to six inches in diameter. They are deck fillers and most cruising boats have at least one each for water, waste and fuel. They should be labeled. A deck fitting key, screw driver or winch handle may be needed to open the filler by turning it counterclockwise.

Deck fillers for water and fuel provide an opening through which tanks below are filled. Waste, on the other hand, empties through the filler. A hose attaches to the filler and a vacuum pump draws waste from the holding tank. Most boaters prefer to leave this task to experts who may be found at pump-out

These dual bow rollers are molded into the stem fitting.

A deck filler used for filling fresh water tanks.

stations on municipal or fuel docks or on a work boat which can make periodic visits. Improper use of self-operated pump-out facilities could result in serious environmental and health consequences. Secure proper instruction before pumping a holding tank yourself.

THE COCKPIT

Small boat sailors may discover more unfamiliar territory in the cockpit of a cruising sailboat than anywhere else on deck. Some modern sailboat designs boast that every sailing operation can be performed from the cockpit. Safety and convenience make the cockpit an ideal place to spend most of your time above deck.

The winches you mastered as a small boat sailor may have some puzzling new features. Self tailing winches eliminate the chore of tailing or pulling a line with one hand while grinding the winch with the other. Winches are wrapped clockwise, as usual. When enough coils have been placed on the drum, pass the tail through the crooked metal feeder near the top of the winch. Then pull the tail securely into the self tailing jaws at the top of the winch which holds the line in place, much like a clam cleat. The line will not slip out of the groove if it has been inserted securely. This leaves your tailing hand free to help grind the winch or balance yourself on the deck.

Silver feeder arm guides a jib sheet into the self tailing jaws that hold it securely.

Larger winches with greater pulling power may also have more than one speed. A winch handle turns a small winch clockwise while clicking freely on a ratchet when turned to the left. Two speed winches turn when the handle moves in either direction. The reverse action of the winch handle causes the winch to continue turning clockwise only slower and with less effort. Gear reduction inside the winch makes this possible. There may also be a switch on the winch which activates a further gear reduction and takes less effort to turn when the winch is loaded.

(A) mainsheet, (B) traveler, (C) hydraulic control panel and (D) instruments are typically found in the cockpit area.

INSTRUMENTS

Cockpit instruments deliver navigation and safety information to the helmsman and navigator. Attention to details such as compass course, speed and depth becomes more critical as we wander further from home port. Navigation would be more difficult and much less precise without the information these exceptionally reliable instruments provide.

The compass should already be familiar. The Sailing Skills portion of Section III covers the fine art of sailing a compass course. The compass sits on the binnacle, a metal structure rising from the cockpit sole which supports the steering wheel, gear shift and throttle. An inverted "U" shaped stainless steel tube, running between the forward part of the binnacle and the cockpit sole, may be used to provide added stability. It makes a great hand hold and may also be used to mount a small cockpit table. The wheel brake, a large knob attached to the binnacle, tensions the steering mechanism making the wheel more difficult to turn. It comes in handy when the helmsman must leave the helm for a short period of time.

A lever is often mounted on either side of the binnacle. The throttle controls engine speed and the shifter engages forward, neutral and reverse. More on this later.

Storage compartments lie beneath some or all of the cockpit seats. Hinges and latches help identify which seats hide lockers. Simply lift the seats to reveal the cavity below. These lockers make great storage areas for items which are likely to be used on deck. Outboard engine and stove fuel should not be stored in closed compartments. If fuel has been stored in these lockers take extra care to ventilate them. Emergency equipment such as PFDs and distress signals should be placed where they are immediately accessible in case of emergency. Also, packing the largest, heaviest or least often used items on the bottom will prevent a great deal of struggling later in your voyage.

The engine controls are found near the wheel. Starting and stopping mechanisms along with water temperature, battery charging, oil pressure and fuel tank level may be on this panel depending on the manufacturer and type of engine. Diesel engines may also have a glow plug which heats the inside of the cylinder, making the engine easier to start.

Most cruising sailboats have two separate electrical systems. The house or DC system operates everything which can be used while underway including lights, electronics, bilge pumps, etc. Power comes from batteries which work much like a car battery. The auxiliary or AC system powers the battery charger, water heater, refrigeration and wall outlets.

A shore power cable energizes the AC system at the dock. It stretches between a dock outlet and a receptacle somewhere in the cockpit area. Always switch the circuit breaker on the dock to "off" before attaching or removing the cable. Where circuit breakers are not mounted, disconnect the shore end of the cable first. Re-connect by attaching the boat end of the cable first. Remove the cable by turning the outer rim of the cable end counter clockwise until it is freed from the threaded lip on the receptacle. Then turn the cable end itself counter clockwise and pull it off. It should only turn a fraction of a turn. A cap will fall into place, which then tightens over the three exposed prongs.

Look for a manual bilge pump usually mounted somewhere, either in a cockpit locker, through the locker and into the cockpit or on the cockpit sole. It either has a handle molded onto it or a detachable handle which fits into a socket on the pump. The pump's discharge hose attaches to a fitting which passes through the hull, a through-hull fitting. The intake hose leads to a pick-up fitting in the bilge. (More on through-hulls and the bilge in Section II.) Vigorous pumping on either type of pump will start water flow if the bilge is sufficiently full.

Chains, gears, cables or sometimes hydraulics connect the wheel on the binnacle with the rudder. Occasionally, the machinery breaks down and the wheel becomes inoperable. An emergency tiller is provided for such occasions. Locate the rudder post extension to prepare for emergency tiller exercises later. It is positioned on the center line usually aft of the binnacle. It may sit beneath an aft locker known as a lazarette or under a deck cap which can be easily opened by turning it counterclockwise. In boats with an aft cabin it may be under the berth in the aft cabin.

Like the bow, the stern area is cordoned off with a pulpit. The stern pulpit usually supports a swim ladder which can be lowered to retrieve swimmers or help people in and out of the dinghy. Swim ladders should be raised while underway.

Horseshoe shaped, Type IV, throwable PFDs often rest in a wire frame which is attached to the stern pulpit. Make sure the horseshoe is secure enough to stay attached yet can be easily removed in an emergency.

A fresh water washdown system consisting of a nozzle and a flexible hose may also be located in the stern area. Use it to wash salt from people and gear on their way back aboard after swimming. Water pressure comes from either a switch on the DC panel or a foot pump.

This concludes our tour of the deck. Later in the text we take a closer look at the operation of many things we have just examined. Becoming familiar with the names, functions and location of everything on deck is an important first step to mastering a new boat.

(A) Shore power receptacle and (B) Stern pulpit

CLOTHING AND PERSONAL GEAR

One of the many ironies of sailboat cruising is that you need a greater variety of clothing but your volume of personal gear must remain limited to match the available storage space. Only in guaranteed awful weather (and who wants to sail then anyway?) may you exclude one type of apparel — your warm weather clothes. Otherwise, smart planners pack for the best, the worst and everything in between.

Lists of personal gear will vary greatly from individual to individual. Each sailor should make a list of personal needs. Compile the list well in advance and review it before packing time to allow for adding or deleting gear. It might seem unbelievable that someone could forget to pack something as important as a checkbook or a swim suit; but in the heat of the last minute dash to get out the door anything can happen. The list-making procedure helps avoid these problems. Some of the following suggestions may be helpful in creating your personal list.

Foul weather gear, hat and gloves ensure comfort during periods of inclement weather.

HYGIENE/MEDICINE

Start with the things which take up the least space. Toothpaste, toothbrush and comb are easy to remember but also easy to replace. Prescription drugs or contact lens solution may not be as easily replaced. Unlike a hotel, a boat may not provide soap and shampoo. If your dreams of sunshine are fulfilled you will need skin protection appropriate for your coloring. Pack lip protection and, in the event the sun block proves to be less than total, sunburn cream. Consolidate non-prescription drugs such as aspirin or allergy capsules in one bottle. Avoid packing large containers of things such as

mouthwash and hand cream. Small, plastic bottles with screw off caps help keep the volume of supplies consistent with the duration of the trip.

Other Suggested Personal Items
- Camera and film
- Reading material
- Towels
- Small flashlight
- Sunglasses on a lanyard
  (spare pair in case one falls overboard)
- Knife
- Sewing kit
- Small zip-top plastic bags
- Packet of laundry soap and coins for washers

CLOTHING

Many sailors go a little "overboard" in this department. Begin your list by selecting clothing for each category of weather; cold, rain, cool, hot. Add to this any special activities you may plan; jogging, hiking, snorkeling, fishing.

Begin with "cold" and list the things which make sense just for that weather condition.

COLD
- Insulated jacket
- Sweater
- Jeans
- Long underwear
- Wool socks
- Hats (for warmth)
- Gloves (for warmth and protection)

RAIN
- Hat with visor
- Gloves
- Foul weather jacket w/hood
- Foul weather pants (weight according to season)
- Foul weather boots
- Neck towel; a small terry towel to absorb water that enters your suit at the neck.

Note: Foul weather gear deposits all of its accumulated rain water where the protection ends. If you cover up from head to ankles and omit the boots because of the season, your shoes will collect the water that falls on your entire body. Wet shoes, regardless of temperature, are no fun.

Continue with logical items in the other categories. Once the list looks complete, review it to consolidate and eliminate non-essential items. When the list has been purged place numbers beside each item to indicate how many are necessary.

As a final check, see if some items might be able to do double duty. Could you hike in your running shoes? Could a foul weather gear top double as a jacket? Capilene and polypro are examples of light weight synthetic insulating fabrics that work well in the marine environment. Cotton absorbs water and may be a poor choice.

Avoid the temptation to toss out necessary items in the name of saving space. The process of streamlining a list should only help to identify superfluous items.

Travel by sailboat opens up a world which most people only occasionally earn the privilege of visiting. Discomfort from the elements can change the most fascinating adventure into a tortuous nightmare. Packing well can make all the difference.

REVIEW QUESTIONS

1. The main halyard always exits the

_____ part of the masthead.

2. The_____ runs below the lifelines along the entire perimeter of the deck.

3. The forestay attaches to the hull by means of a

_____

4. _____ for water and fuel provide an opening through which tanks below are filled.

5. The _____, a large knob attached to the binnacle, tensions the steering mechanism making the wheel more difficult to turn.

Circle the correct true or false answers below

6. True or False?   The rudder post on a yawl is forward of the mizzen mast.

7. True or False?   Hydraulic backstays and boom vangs use an electric pump for pressurization.

8. True or False?   Towing lines should not pass through bow fairleads.

9. True or False?   Always turn the circuit breaker on the dock to "off" before disconnecting the shore power.

10. True or False?   The "house" electrical system is also called the AC system.

SAILING SKILLS

Sailing attracts intelligent, active people because it blends intellectual activity with a physical challenge to produce a highly pleasurable, rewarding experience. In other words, it's fun.

Both theory and manual skills combine to form the masterpiece known as an "accomplished sailor". The following "Sailing Skills" can only be properly acquired after sufficiently repeating each skill. These exercises are meant to be performed, not just studied.

SAFETY EQUIPMENT

You have already become familiar with the United States Coast Guard's minimum requirements for safety gear on smaller boats. Many of the requirements for larger boats are the same; while some of the following information is new. Make sure to locate and inspect each item listed below. Demonstrate the operation of each safety item for everyone on board. Also, use the rules to determine which items are required for your dinghy.

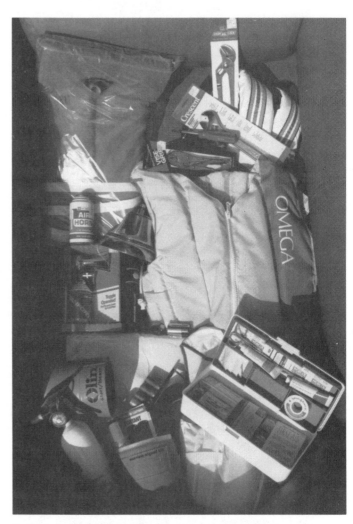

Sailors should augment required items with other important items which are not specified in Coast Guard regulations.

PFDs

One type I, II, III, IV or V PFD per person must be on board any boat less than 16 feet in length. Boats 16 feet and longer must have one type I, II, III or V on board for each person. Type V PFDs are only acceptable when they are being worn. Names have been given to these four types of PFD which reflect the conditions and waters for which they are appropriate. Type I: Offshore Life Jacket, Type II: Nearshore Buoyancy Vest, Type III: Flotation Aid and Type V: Hybrid Jacket. Check the tag on the PFD to determine its type.

The tag also has information on weight and chest size tolerances. Children should have PFDs which are approved for their weight and size. Assuming that "more is better" could be a costly mistake. A poor fitting PFD could slip entirely off the child's body. Also, brief kids on how to don a life preserver. A practice swim is advisable. The panic which comes with suddenly being thrust into cold water might cause violent thrashing of the arms and legs resulting in forces counter to the righting effect of the PFD. Children should be told to remain calm and swim normally.

One Type IV throwable PFD must be on board any vessel 16 feet and longer. You may have already located the horseshoe ring on the stern pulpit. You may also find a cushion, about 16 inches square, which qualifies as a Type IV. Check the tags for verification of type and approval.

Horseshoe shaped Type IV PFDs are common on cruising sailboats.

SIGNALS

Vessels less than 40 feet are not specifically required to carry a whistle, horn or bell. However, the navigation rules require sound signals under certain circumstances, thus implying the need for a horn. Vessels 40 feet or more are required to carry a power whistle or power horn. Compressed gas powered horns are most popular. The gas becomes a liquid under pressure. Shaking the canister can help determine its level. A thin, plastic diaphragm makes the sound in most models. New horns come with a spare. Keep an eye on it and take a moment to study its installation.

Boats over 40 feet in length must have a Ship's Bell onboard. Its sounding indicates that a boat is anchored in fog. It should not be used as a sound-making device while underway in restricted visibility.

Three daytime and three nighttime visual distress signals must be kept onboard at all times. You know from basic sailing that a daytime flare gives off smoke and a nighttime flare glows. The two most common types are hand held or aerial pyrotechnic flares. Both types come with directions printed on the package. Hold hand-held flares downwind and away from the boat and crew. Fire aerial flares in an arc which will deliver them downwind of the boat. Also, flares have expiration dates and must be kept up to date. Check types, dates and make sure everyone on board knows how to operate visual distress signals. Recreational boats less than 16 feet are exempt from flare requirements.

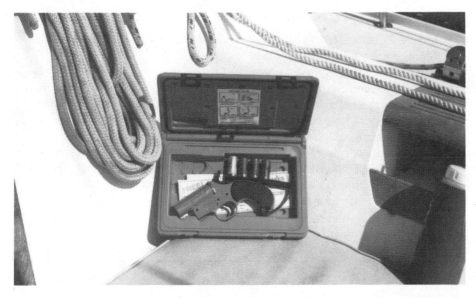

Aerial flares are launched from a special pistol.

FIRE EXTINGUISHER(S)

Fire Extinguishers are not optional because every boat in the size category covered by this book carries at least one type of petroleum based fuel. You must have one B-I ("B"=type of fire it is rated to fight, I= capacity) on vessels less than 26 feet. Vessels 26 to 40 feet require one B-II or two B-I extinguishers. Three B-I or one B-II and one B-I extinguishers must be on board boats 40 to 65 feet. Fire extinguishers discharge by pressing together the two handles on top. They should be fired in short bursts at the base of a flame. Check the gauge to determine whether the extinguisher is charged.

ENGINE STARTING

The inboard engine was arguably the most important innovation in sailing history. Purists who regard it as a noisy little nuisance usually soften their stand when presented with the alternative of sailing in and out of the harbor. The calming elixir of travel by sail can turn to unrelenting annoyance while sitting becalmed for hours on end. The inboard, auxiliary engine saves us from ourselves in such cases. It also gives sailors the option of maintaining a schedule, if they so desire.

Section II takes us through a close inspection of the engine. The following exercise will teach just enough to get it safely started.

1. **Determine whether the auxiliary engine runs on gasoline or diesel fuel.** Deck fillers may give a clue but they could be wrong. An owner's manual, if available, will provide fairly reliable information. Section II provides a fool-proof visual way to identify the type of fuel.

2. **Locate the main battery switch down below and turn it to "All" or "Both".** This sends battery power to the starter and blower.

3. **Locate the "Blower" or "Bilge Blower" switch either on the main switch panel or the engine control panel in the cockpit.** Turn it on. Let it run for five minutes.
Gasoline fumes are heavier than air and extremely combustible. A bilge blower, which acts as an exhaust fan for the bilge, must be operated for at least five minutes prior to starting the engine. Diesel fumes are much less volatile but, if gasoline for the outboard or liquified petroleum gas for the galley stove are present, dangerous fumes could still settle in the bilge. Always run the blower before starting the engine.   *(continued)*

OTHER REQUIREMENTS

Gasoline powered vessels must have a back fire flame arrestor on the carburetor which prevents flames from escaping in the event of a backfire. Gas powered vessels also have very specific ventilation requirements. Sailors operating vessels with gas engines should check the appropriate U. S. government publications or contact the local Coast Guard office for detailed specifications. Charterers will very rarely encounter a gasoline powered vessel in a major charter fleet.

By now you should recognize that these are minimum requirements and supplemental equipment is necessary to ensure safety. Though not intended for crew safety, other requirements should be noted.

An approved marine sanitation device must be used on all vessels with installed toilet facilities. The holding tank, which we will look at more closely later, qualifies for this regulation.

State registration numbers must be displayed plainly on the hull unless the vessel is documented, a procedure which registers the vessel with the Coast Guard. Ship's papers must also be kept on board.

The person who assumes responsibility for the boat takes responsibility for compliance with these regulations. Wise sailors will know the rules and abide by them.

4. **Verify that the gear shift is in neutral.** The gear shift snaps gently into and out of gear while the throttle travels from the slowest setting to the fastest setting with uniform resistance. Finding neutral should be easy after pushing the shift and throttle all the way forward and back a few times. If two levers are not present for the throttle and shift, a single lever control system could be mounted in the cockpit. It consists of a lever and a button. The lever acts only as a throttle when the button is activated. The transmission stays in neutral. Push the button in and the lever controls both shifting and engine speed. Follow the directions for the throttle in Step 5 with the button out. Perform the "Gear check" described below to clarify the button and lever functions.

5. **Set the throttle about halfway between where it stops in both directions.**

6. **Locate the engine fuel shut-off lever.** There may be a small handle which pulls out and pushes back in. Look around the engine control panel or in the lazarette. It must be pushed in before the engine will start.

7. **Locate the "Glow Plug" or pre-heater if the engine comes equipped with one.** It may have its own switch or it may work by turning the key in one direction or the other. It probably needs the key turned "on", one click to the right, if it has a separate switch. When the key goes to the "on" position a buzzer should sound. It indicates a lack of oil pressure. A similar alarm sounds when the engine heats excessively. It should stop when the engine starts. 20 seconds seems to be the standard prescription for glow plug operating time.

8. **Start the engine.** Either operate the starter by turning the key beyond "on", like a car, or by pressing a separate button near the key. Stand by to back off the throttle in case the engine races. If the engine fails to start after a few tries of less than 10 seconds each, try advancing the throttle. Otherwise, repeat steps 7 and 8. Avoid cranking the engine excessively. If it will not start, then something substantial is wrong. The examination of the engine in Section II and Section V, Troubleshooting, may help in determining the cause of your engine's malady. The buzzer should stop within seconds after the engine comes to life. Take a look at the gauges on the control panel. The ammeter should stand somewhere around 12 to 14 volts if the battery is charging. The water temperature gauge should point to the lowest level and can rise as far as 200°-210° without cause for alarm. Oil Pressure of 40-80 pounds per square inch is fine. Once the engine has started, check the exhaust discharge to make sure that water flows out with the exhaust.

This indicates that cooling water is flowing through the engine. If exhaust smoke escapes without water, turn the engine off immediately. Something is very wrong. Section II and Section V provide information which may solve the problem.

GEAR CHECK

Once the engine has begun running smoothly, idle it back as far as possible without stalling. Somewhere around 500 RPMs on the tachometer should be comfortable. Slip the shift into gear momentarily, then shift back to neutral. Note the direction you shifted; forward, aft, up or down (this will depend on how the shift is mounted on the binnacle). Then notice the resulting movement of the boat. The dock lines should strain to keep the boat from moving either backward or forward. Try shifting in the other direction and make a mental note of the results. Eliminate the guess work about which way to shift and you eliminate potential mistakes when the boat is underway.

PREPARING DEPARTURE

Believe it or not, more damage occurs to boats in marinas than on the open sea. If a sailboat's maneuverability were compared to that of a land vehicle, it would probably resemble one of those old fashioned bicycles with the giant wheel in the front. It doesn't begin moving quickly, it has no brakes and once you get on it you really have to plan ahead to get off safely.

Simply stated, the major challenge of docking and undocking is to do so without causing injury or damage. Everything else is considered finesse. The following concepts will help you avoid injury and damage and begin to develop finesse.

PROPELLER FORCES

A propeller works like a screw, burrowing itself into a piece of wood. Every time the screw turns, it moves further into the wood. Turn the other way and the screw retreats.

The propeller, spinning hundreds of times a minute, wants to go through the water like the screw goes into the wood. It cannot move, however, unless the entire boat comes along for the ride. The bulk of the boat somewhat dampens the initial effectiveness of the propeller revolutions, but the propeller ultimately moves through the water as the boat gains headway. A household fan is really nothing more than a propeller turning through air. Like a fan, a propeller has blades, usually two or three. A close inspection of the fan will reveal that the blades are angled in relation to the shaft to which they are attached. That angle is called pitch and, without it the screwing action is lost, and you have no propeller. Flat fan blades, like a dinner plate with slots cut into it, could spin forever and never cool you down.

DIRECTION OF ROTATION

Some propellers are designed to move forward through the water when they rotate clockwise; they are called right handed props. Propellers with the blades angled in the opposite direction must rotate counterclockwise to move ahead and are called left handed props. Owners' manuals often provide this information, but it is best to watch the direction that the propeller shaft (examined in the next section) spins while the transmission is shifted to forward.

PROP WALK

There are additional forces produced by a spinning propeller. Think of the propeller as a wheel with a solid surface below it. Looking at the stern of the boat; if the wheel turns clockwise it will move to the right. If it turns counter clockwise it moves to the left.

The propeller's pitch causes a propeller to pull the stern of the boat in the same direction the wheel would travel. The tendency is commonly called prop walk. Prop walk occurs whenever the propeller is turning but it is most noticeable in reverse.

The information above should lead you to conclude that in reverse a right handed prop will kick the stern to port, and that a left handed prop will draw the stern to starboard. The most profound effects of prop walk come in the period between the time the boat is at rest and the time it has gained enough speed to have the rudder become effective, which is known as steerage way.

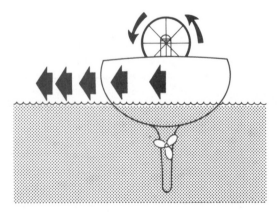

A propeller turning counter-clockwise in reverse pulls the boat's stern to port.

LEAVING A SLIP

More helping hands make most jobs aboard a sailboat easier and casting off is certainly no exception. It can be accomplished alone, but assigning crew to tasks makes it a lot less taxing.

1. **Determine wind direction.** Until the boat achieves enough speed to counteract the effects of the wind, it presents large surfaces on which the wind can push. Wind asserts its most dramatic effect during the period of time when you are broadside, or perpendicular to it. Small boats were easy to fend off but a forty foot boat drifting sideways at a half knot takes much more power to stop. Trace the course that the boat will follow on the way out of the slip. Anticipate when the boat will be most vulnerable and in what direction it will be pushed. Also keep in mind that the boat tends to back into the wind. The boat will try to point toward the direction from which the wind blows as you gather sternway.

2. **Check for rate and direction of current.** Watch debris on the water's surface or check to see if eddies occur around pilings or on the corners of docks. Estimate the

direction that the combined force of wind and current would push the boat. The judgement necessary to make graceful departures and landings comes from practice. Begin to develop your judgement by observing, estimating and being careful.

3. **Cast off extra lines.** Start with the ones which have least strain. Keeping the boat straight in the slip is of prime concern, especially in windy conditions. Position the boat snug to the dock on the side closer to the direction the bow must point when leaving the slip area. In other words, pull the hull close to the dock opposite the direction the stern will back toward. Suspend the boat snugly between a bow and a stern line.

4. **Begin moving aft.** Cast off the bow and stern lines starting with those that are not under strain. Shift into reverse and add enough throttle to get the boat moving. Greater opposing wind strength and current requires more power. Shift back to neutral once the boat begins making way.

There are two critical factors which will ensure success in this maneuver. First, the boat must stay straight in the slip until the beam has cleared the outside corners of the slip. Second, the bow must then swing one way and the stern the other to set the boat up to head out of the slip area. The rudder may not render enough steerage to guarantee your control if prop walk, wind and current exert opposing forces. You may find that you need other assistance.

Here are a few suggestions.

BOW CREW

This individual can keep the boat straight by holding and adjusting "walking" bow lines. The crew walks the boat back with the dockline in hand and attached to the bow. Soon the rudder may be effective enough to control the boat's movement. The lines are then thrown onto the dock and a boat hook is used to continue guiding the vessel. Alternatively, the person on the bow might also hold and adjust a bow spring line in conjunction with a crew member on the stern. The spring line remains within the bowman's reach for a longer time than the bow lines, creating an advantage of longer usefulness. It does, however require another person.

STERN CREW

This person retains control of either a stern spring line or a stern line. It must be attached to the dock on the side that the stern will point when it first turns in the fairway. When the bow crew has cast off his line and the beam has cleared the slip entrance, the stern crew can tension his line on a cleat or winch aft of the boat's radius or pivot point. The line's tension draws the stern in the desired direction. Make sure that there are no knots in the line and it is free to run when the time comes to cast it off. Also, it must be 1 1/2 to 2 boat lengths long.

Another possibility is the running spring or dock line. One end is made fast on a stern cleat. The other end passes around a dock cleat or piling and back on board to the stern area. Tensioning occurs as it did in the previous example. The stern crew casts off the running end and quickly gathers the line from the other end.

We never choose to place a line in the water with the propeller engaged. Unfortunately, the running spring line forces us to choose between maneuverability and the remote chance that the line will foul the propeller during the few seconds it remains water bound. Minimize the risk by casting off and retrieving the line during the time that the boat glides in neutral (Step 6).

5. **The helmsman negotiates the turn.** The wheel turns in the direction which the stern will turn. Imagine the same maneuver in a car and turn the boat the same way.

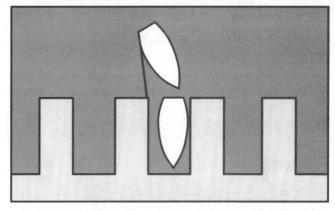

(1) The boat is pulled close to the dock opposite the direction it will turn. (2) A stern spring line helps the crew manually turn the boat in the proper direction at the right time.

6. **Shift to neutral, then to forward.** You may have had to go back into reverse after shifting to neutral In Step 4 or you may have remained in reverse to overcome wind and/or current. Once the boat has cleared the slip and any other obstacles, begin moving ahead. Drift for as short a time as possible.

7. **Turn the wheel back in the other direction.** Anticipate where you want to turn the wheel even before the boat has steerage way. In a tight space turning the wrong direction, even for a few seconds, can spell disaster.

Speed in tight places and swimming with sharks have one important thing in common, they can both result in pain. Rather than add a little speed to slide out of imminent contact with another object, go into neutral or add power in the other direction to slow down and fend off. We try to avoid hitting anything but even the most experienced skippers are no match for the demented will of a sailboat traveling in reverse.

Assign one or more crew members to patrol the deck with the biggest fenders aboard. They can slip quickly between your boat and another object long enough to get things under control and make a plan to get moving. Wind and current may call for turning the propeller faster but your best course is to keep the boat moving slowly and under control. Even the wound to your pride will be smaller if your mishaps occur while traveling slowly.

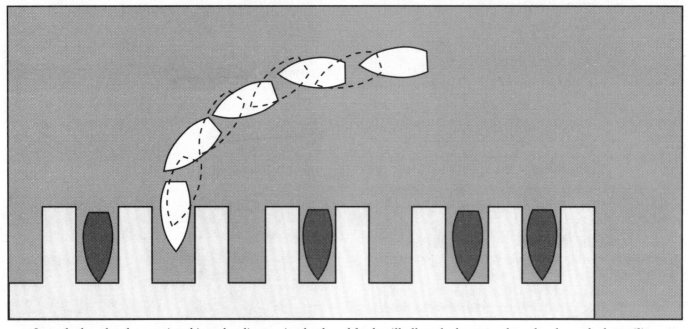

Once the bow has been pointed into the slip, turning back and forth will allow the beam to clear the closer dock or piling.

RETURNING TO THE SLIP

The same forces prevail during slip re-entry.

1. **Assess wind and current forces to predict how they will effect the boat.**

2. **Adjust the boat's position in the waterway accordingly.** In a waterway with boat slips on both sides, imagine a line dividing the channel in half just like the lines on a highway. Position the boat in the middle of the lane opposite your slip. Glide along in neutral and try to feel whether the wind and current are having any effect. If so, move to one side or the other of the lane but remain on your half of the waterway. Avoid getting too close to the slips on the outside of your lane. When you turn to enter the slip, the bow turns toward the slip; but the stern also turns in the opposite direction. Travel too close to the outside and it may be impossible to turn when the time comes.

3. **Begin making an arc toward the slip.** Moving just fast enough to maintain steerage way, estimate when the bow is about a slip and a half away from your intended destination. Work to position the boat so it enters the slip straight. This is often easier said than done. You know that part of the boat will go into the slip because the bow is pointing between the two docks or pilings. The boat's final position in the slip can be adjusted with muscle power and dock lines, if necessary.

The beam suddenly becomes a nuisance. It can smash into the approaching corner of the slip if you enter at too wide

an angle. Once the bow is pointing into the slip, begin a process of turning into and away from the slip. In other words, point the bow directly at the corner of the outside dock for a moment, then turn into the slip. Repeat this as many times as necessary to clear the beam around the closer corner of the slip. This turning maneuver is unnecessary in a wide waterway because the boat can line up directly across from the slip and come in straight.

A crew member should be stationed at the beam facing forward with a bow spring line in one hand and a shroud for balance in the other. Regardless of the position of the bow, when the boat enters the slip the beam will eventually come close to the dock. Docking crew should step over the lifeline and onto the middle of the dock; never jump. The line can then wrap around the end of a cleat midway along the dock and be used to slow the boat down. If the boat has come to rest partially outside the slip the same line can be led to a cleat at the inside end of the slip and help to pull the boat in the rest of the way. A stern crew can step onto the dock when the stern approaches the dock. The same process can be executed on the other side as long as the other dock sits close enough to the boat to step onto it.

STOPPING THE ENGINE

When the boat is secured, stop the engine by pulling out the fuel shut-off handle until the engine dies. The alarm will sound until you turn the key off. Engines without fuel shut-off levers stop by pulling the throttle all the way toward "slow". Once the engine stops, return the fuel shut-off lever to the normal operating position so the engine will be ready to start again.

RAISING SAILS

Thus far you have identified the running rigging for both the main sail and the jib. Despite past experience with smaller boats, a world of mystery could lie concealed by these sails. Now is a good time to explore this new territory.

You have already checked the wind direction. During the motoring exercise leaving and returning to the slip, plan to dock the boat with the bow upwind. Perhaps, with luck, the bow points to windward in the slip. Otherwise, find an empty slip or dock to commandeer for a short time.

With the dock lines secure and the bow into the wind, run through the familiar process of raising the main.

1. **Take a strain on the topping lift to support the boom as the sail goes up.**

2. **Attach the halyard to the headboard.** Release it from the cleat.

3. **Release the main sheet, boom vang and cunningham.** Alert the crew that the boom is free.

4. **Raise the mainsail.** Watch to see that the luff runs smoothly in its track or groove. A sail is probably stuck when it suddenly becomes difficult to raise. Avoid using the winch for anything other than helping to overcome the steady addition of weight as more sail cloth becomes airborne.

5. **Adjust luff tension.** Tighten the halyard until one or two wrinkles form running parallel along the mast.

6. **Secure and coil the halyard.** Any excess cable should be coiled on the winch drum. Never secure cable to a cleat.

7. **Adjust the topping lift.** Once the sail goes up the topping lift may still hold the boom up. Find the cleat and release the line until a few inches of slack appear when the weight of the boom rests entirely on the sail.

Watch for taught reefing lines as the headboard approaches the masthead. The sail may have been reefed the last time it was lowered. You will get a more in depth look at reefing in Section III.

Every control for the mainsail becomes exposed once the sail has been raised. Raising the sail at the dock gives you plenty of time to follow every line and locate every cleat without the pressure of traffic and navigating.

JIBS

Cruising boats without roller furling follow the same jib raising procedure as their smaller relatives. Attach the tack, the hanks and the halyard. Tie on the sheets and lead them to the cockpit. Then fold the sail as neatly as possible into the bow pulpit. Make sure it takes up as little room on the deck as possible until the time comes to raise sails.

Headfoil systems appear as boats become larger and more sophisticated. A headfoil is a metal or plastic sleeve which fits over the forestay and covers its entire length. One or two tracks or slots run from the bottom to the top of the headfoil. The width of the tracks equals the thickness of about two layers of sail cloth.

The bolt rope, a round plastic cable, is sewn into the leading edge of the jib's luff and it runs from tack to head. The track has a feeder, a wider section of the slot, at the bottom. The bolt rope can be fed inside the track through the feeder. There may also be a pre-feeder to guide the bolt rope into the feeder. It may be molded onto the headfoil or dangle from a short lanyard. Lead the bolt rope through the pre-feeder, the feeder and into the headfoil. Start feeding at the head. As the sail goes up, the bolt rope, which is much wider than the slot, runs inside the headfoil. The limited width of the track keeps the sail attached because the bolt rope is too wide to pull out through the track. Headfoils keep uniform pressure on the luff, allowing smoother air flow over the jib.

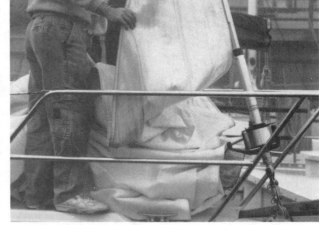

The bolt rope (top) is aligned for its entry into the headfoil. Crew members work the jib into its headfoil by hand before the halyard takes it the rest of the way to the masthead.

ROLLER FURLING

You have already been introduced to the roller furling jib and its parts. Sitting at the dock you have a wonderful opportunity to see how it works.

Ideally, the jib would be set after the main was raised in irons and the boat began to sail close hauled under main alone. The jib would then set to leeward, clear of the mast and rigging. For the purpose of experimentation you can unfurl it with the bow into the wind.

1. **Release both jib sheets.** Make sure the sheets are not coiled, wrapped around winches or secured to cleats.

2. **Uncoil and release the furling line.** Some furling lines are just one long loop which passes over a sheave at the base of the roller furler and attaches to a cleat in the cockpit area. Release the line from its cleat. Others have a single line which rolls up on a drum at the base of the furler when the sail is set. (unfurled). The tail of this line collects in the cockpit area when the sail is furled. Make sure that the line is free to run and that it has been cast off its cleat.

3. **Gently pull the leeward sheet to start the sail unfurling.** In this case there will be no leeward sheet, so choose whichever sheet is convenient. Once the sail has rolled out a few feet the wind usually brings it out the rest of the way. Keep a light strain on the furling line so it wraps smoothly on the furling drum. If it fouls it may need to be pulled in slightly to untangle a knot.

4. **Secure the furling line to its cleat and coil any remaining line.** Because the jib is already raised even when it has been furled, the jib halyard was set, secured and coiled prior to raising the mainsail. Trace the halyard and inspect the sail itself. Some roller furlers have internal halyards but they usually appear on smaller boats. Slack the halyard to drop the sail on deck and then hoist it again. If the roller furling fails, you will need to know how to drop the sail just as if it were any other jib.

Furl the jib by pulling on the furling line. At the same time, ease out both jib sheets, keeping a light strain to make the sail roll up smoothly. Draw it in until the sail is entirely rolled or the drum runs out of line. Some roller furling jibs have enough furling line on the drum to pull a few wraps of the jib sheets around the furled sail. Secure the furling line to its cleat. Secure the sheets to the winches or cleats using mild tension. Nine times out of ten, trouble with roller furling occurs at the drum or somewhere along the path of the furling line. Never force the sail either in or out. Winching in the roller furler might be necessary on very large boats but always avoid using a winch to get a sail unstuck. Roller furlers get easier to operate as the exposed sail area decreases. If the sail becomes harder to furl part way through the furling process, something is caught or binding. Locate and correct the problem rather than forcing it with a winch.

The furling line attaches to an empty drum when the sail is furled.

SUMMARY

Sailing any boat has a lot in common with building or creating an object with your hands. First you must know which tool performs what task. Next you learn how your tools transform the object being built. Then through practice, you gain proficiency with the tools and are able to create a quality finished product.

Each part of the boat which performs a task is one of the tools of sailing. The advantage of small boat experience makes moving into a larger boat an easier transition. Section I has focused on some of the tools necessary to operate a 30 to 50 foot cruising sailboat. The Sailing Skills exercises teach the results of applying the tools to operation of the boat. Use *Cruising Fundamentals* in conjunction with a boat, either in a class or on your own, and part of the building process will be satisfactorily completed. The remaining element, practice, is the only thing preventing you from becoming a satisfied, competent sailor. Take time to practice and you will acquire that sought-after, yet elusive, commodity we call confidence.

GETTING FAMILIAR

"But if you live in the forecastle, you are "as independent as a wood sawyer's clerk", and are a <u>sailor</u>. You hear sailors' talk, learn their ways, their peculiarities of feeling as well as speaking and acting; and, moreover, pick up a great deal of curious and useful information in seamanship, ship's customs, foreign countries, etc., from their long yarns and equally long disputes."

Two Years Before the Mast
— Richard Henry Dana, Jr.

One of the profound differences between day sailing and cruising is found in the relationship between the boat and its crew. Previously, the boat kept people out of the water, moved them from one place to another and provided recreation along the way. Cruising boats take on some formidable added responsibility. In a very real sense, your cruising boat provides for your very survival whenever you leave the harbor.

Your food, water, shelter and ability to communicate with the outside world all come from the boat. It is, in fact, an island; a very barren island except for the things you stock on board prior to sailing. Sailing Knowledge in Section II brings you below deck to explore and master the systems and spaces which help keep you safe and content while underway. Sailing Skills builds on the motoring experience gained from the previous exercises.

Below Deck

We began our topside tour at the bow, so down below we will begin all the way forward and work aft.

The forepeak usually houses a cabin. The berth normally takes up all but enough room to turn around with the door closed. Above, you'll find at least one opening hatch for light and air. Apply a little common sense to the handles and knobs and hatch operation requires no explanation.

The forward bulkhead often has a door that gives access to the chain locker. The rode comes down from the foredeck into the locker through a chain pipe.

The bitter end of the anchor rode should attach to a pad eye. Check the integrity of the hardware. The pad eye is there to prevent accidental loss of the bitter end. It is not a strong point and it should not bear the weight of the vessel while anchored. Avoid the temptation to store anything else in the locker since it will foul the rode.

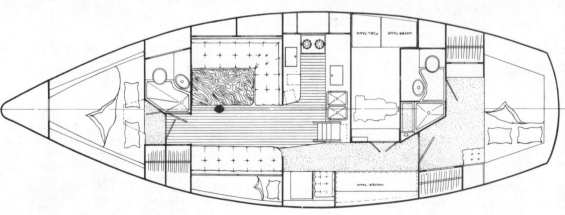

Storage space may include drawers below the berth and/or a hanging locker. Some boats have a section in the middle of the berth which comes out to create more standing room. It lifts in and out of position. Check for latches underneath.

Lifting the cushion will usually reveal removable wooden panel(s). Below you will find more space for storage and perhaps a fitted tank, either plastic or metal. Most likely it holds water, but it could be a sewage holding tank. Follow the large diameter hose from the tank top to the deck fitting to determine the tank's function. You may have already matched the fillers with their purposes. The owner's manual may also provide some important clues.

Check for a removable deck plate covering the bilge. Beneath it you may find empty bilge area or perhaps through-hull fittings, valves which allow water to pass into or out of the boat. Through-hulls come in many shapes and sizes but their function is always the same. Either a lever (seacock) or a screw down faucet type handle (gate valve) can be found somewhere on the side of the fitting. The gate valve works just like a faucet. Turn it off, clockwise, until it stops and water will not flow through the valve. Turn it counter clockwise and it opens the valve and allows water to flow. Turn the seacock handle across or perpendicular to the fitting to close the valve. Water flows when the handle points in the same direction as the fitting.

Any system which requires seawater to flow in or waste water to flow out will have a through-hull. As you learn how everything below deck works, identify items that need a through-hull. Make it your business to locate every through-hull on board and know the system each one serves.

Although usually controlled by the valve, a through-hull is a hole in the boat. Since most through-hulls pick up or discharge below the water line, if the valve or hose leading to it disconnects water will rush into the boat. Attach a soft wood plug, available at most marine stores, to each through-hull. This tapered plug should be forced into the leaking through-hull until water flow stops. Cloth material, rags, a shirt or jacket might also stop a leak when they are jammed into a hole with a screwdriver or similar tool. Water comes through any hole below the waterline with great force and getting anything into a leak will not be easy.

Transducers, sensors which feed information to the instruments, also mount through the hull and may be found in the forward bilge. Knotmeters usually have their sensors mounted forward and on the center line to reduce interference from heeling and disturbed water flow from the keel. Depthsounders function best with their transducers near the center line to reduce inaccuracy caused by heeling. Positioning the depthsounder forward of the keel also helps give early warning of an approaching obstruction.

A removable plug with a paddle wheel at the bottom sends speed information to the knotmeter's speed display unit. Motion through the water makes the wheel spin. Sea life may collect on the transducer and keep the wheel from turning. A round cap, attached to the top of the plug, screws onto the through-hull. Unscrew the cap and pull the plug right out. A fountain of water will pour in when the plug comes out. Another plug, without a paddle wheel, should be attached to the

through-hull or located nearby in the cabin. It has a cap and it screws on the same way and replaces the paddle wheel unit when it is removed.

Depthsounder transducers have no easily removable or repairable parts. The unit sends out and receives high frequency sound pulses. The depthsounder computes the time between transmitting a pulse and receiving its echo and uses it to determine the depth. The transducer requires no maintenance.

The seacock lever in the (top) diagram is parallel to the through-hull fitting indicating it is open.

Below, the lever is perpendicular to the fitting preventing water from flowing through. A soft wood plug has been placed in the fitting to seal a leak caused by a faulty valve.

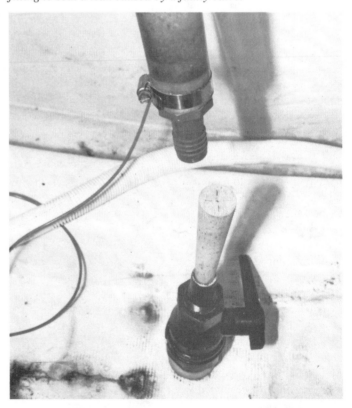

The knot meter transducer can be removed to clean and inspect the paddlewheel.
Depth sounder transducers are not normally serviceable.

THE HEAD

We call the bathroom on board ship the head. Sailors can expect all the services provided by the bathroom at home as long as a few simple rules are observed. "There are no plumbers at sea," is a phrase which has been immortalized in many a marine head. It should serve as a reminder to take care with the temperamental appliances in this tiny cabin.

WATER PRESSURE

Ashore we simply turn on the faucet and out comes an endless supply of clean, clear water. Aboard ship the tanks we may have already seen under the forward bunks hold our entire water supply. An electric pump draws water from the tanks and forces it through lines to all the faucets on board. When pressure has been established in the lines a switch turns the pump off. This switch responds to any drop in pressure by turning the pump back on and restoring fairly stable water pressure. Look for valves that switch between tanks.

SINK

There are no real surprises here. Faucets work like faucets and the drain works like a drain. Follow the drain hose from the bottom of the bowl to its through-hull.

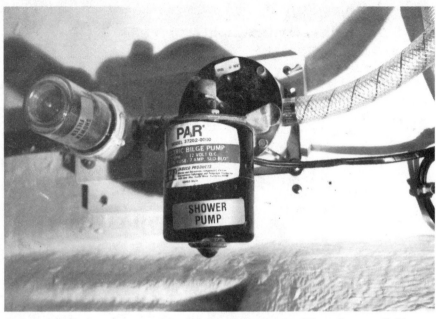

DC electric motors power on-board fresh water pumps. Filter elements (left) remove debris from the water supply and could restrict water flow when debris accumulates.

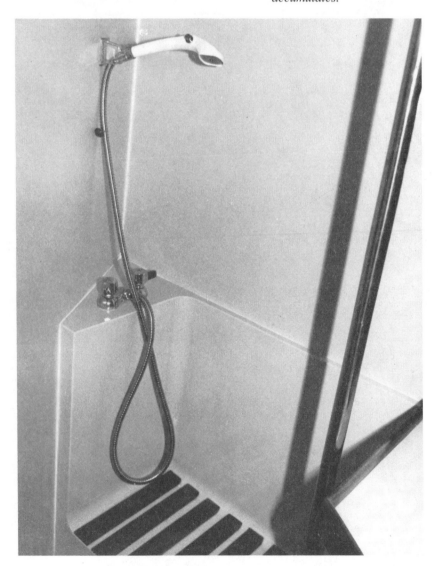

THE SHOWER

Personal hygiene on a sailboat takes determination and perhaps some acrobatic prowess. Most cruising sailboats use a European style, hand held shower head mounted on a flexible hose. Faucets mix hot and cold water that flows to the shower head. Another valve, usually just a sliding pin, starts and stops the water at the shower head. The valve on the shower head helps save water, an important factor in view of our limited supply.

The shower stall, if there is one, may not be tall enough for standing straight. Look for a shower curtain. The space enclosed by drawing it is where the designers intend for you to take a shower. It may just consist of the area between the commode and the sink.

Some showers will drain. This arrangement requires very little attention provided the automatic bilge pump operates correctly. Others drain to a sump, a small reservoir below the shower drain. A switch somewhere in the head compartment operates the sump pump which pumps the water overboard. After a shower run the pump until all the water has been cleared from the sump. The pump spins faster at a higher pitch when it has cleared the sump of water. Some shallow sumps may overflow unless the pump runs during a shower.

MARINE HEAD

There are at least three different items named "head" on a sailboat. The room where the toilet is found and the toilet itself are both called the head. A reference to operating the head can only mean the toilet.

The operating principles of a marine head are simple. Water from outside the boat is pumped through the toilet to flush out the waste. The combined water and waste then either go back out through the hull or into a holding tank. The theory, though simple, often gets complicated when put into practice. Understanding the head and its components can keep your relationship civil and casual.

The working components of the head are a pump handle and a valve. The pump handle usually moves up and down. It performs double duty by pumping water in and pumping the contents of the bowl out. The valve controls water intake. One position, which may be labeled as "flush" or "wet" opens the valve and allows water to come into the bowl with every stroke. The other position, "dry bowl", cuts off the water intake allowing only the pump's discharge function to work.

Water comes to the head through a hose usually an inch or so in diameter. Waste travels out through a thick hose which connects to the bottom of the head and probably disappears through a bulkhead. The plumbing on some boats could win an award for creativity. Hoses and tubes twist and turn through valves, pumps and inaccessible compartments. Follow each hose to determine where it comes from and where it goes. The following definitions should help you decipher the maze of hoses and hardware in the boat's hidden crevices.

Y Valve: If the boat has one, the Y valve will be the first fitting along the discharge hose from the head. Waste enters this valve at one end and is directed out one of two hoses at the other end. One line leads to a through-hull and directly overboard and the other into the holding tank. There may be instructions on the valve itself. Generally, the handle points to the discharge hose that is closed. Some boats have a closed system with no direct overboard discharge from the head, therefore, no Y valve.

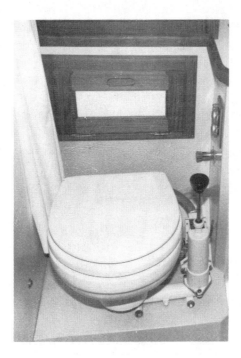

Through-hulls: We have seen these already. The head intake comes through one valve and discharge goes through another. Follow the lines attached to the head and locate both through-hulls.

Holding tank: The remaining discharge line from the Y valve, or the discharge line from the head if there is no Y valve, carries waste to the holding tank. It will be rigid metal or plastic box or a flexible rubber "bladder". A vent line from the top of the tank to an opening on the hull allows air to pass in and out of the tank and allows dangerous methane gas to escape. The vent works very poorly as an overflow for the tank. Avoid testing its overflow capabilities by monitoring tank levels and pumping out often.

Macerator: There may be another line out of the holding tank to give boaters the option of emptying their holding tank themselves. It runs through a pump, either manual or electric, to a through-hull. Open the through-hull and operate the pump. Electric pumps have a switch on the main DC switch panel. Listen for the pump to spin faster and its pitch to rise when the tank is empty. A manual pump will have less resistance when the contents of the tank are gone. Never operate the macerator in lakes or within three miles of shore in coastal waters.

Using the head should be simple and painless as long as you follow these simple steps.

1. **Open through-hulls.** If the holding tank is in use, open only the water intake.
2. **Open the valve.** Place the valve on the toilet itself in the up, "wet" or "flush", position.
3. **Prime the head.** Pump a few strokes to get an inch or so of water in the bowl.
4. **Use the head.**
5. **Pump wet.** Pump with the valve open until the bowl contains only clear water. Extra pumping to clear the lines of waste would be desirable. The limited capacity of most holding tanks make it impractical. Clear the lines in areas beyond the three mile limit where direct overboard or macerator use is permitted.
6. **Pump dry.** Close the head valve and pump until all of the water has been cleared.
7. **Close through-hulls.** Close the valves when the head is not in use.

Through-hulls on some head installations can remain open while underway without any problems. Others allow water to flood the head and the boat under certain conditions. Brief all crew on opening and closing through hulls. Monitor the water level in the head while underway with valves open. Always keep the head valve closed when the head is not in frequent use.

Most head problems occur when objects clog the discharge systems, check valves and piping. Never put anything other than a small amount of toilet paper into the head. EVERYTHING else should be wrapped up and put into the trash.

MAIN CABIN

The largest interior space on the boat is called the main cabin or main saloon. Hatches overhead and ports along the cabin trunk provide ventilation. While exploring any new boat pull out all of the settee cushions and explore the spaces behind and underneath them. Your waste discharge tour may already have taken you under some of the settees. Now, look under the rest. Note the available storage spaces. Longer journeys increase your appreciation of storage space.

Through-hulls and tanks may be located in these storage spaces. Locate their sources as you did earlier in the section.

Look closely at the settees without their cushions. They often convert to double berths. In some cases, the board beneath the cushions slides out to create a wider platform. Quite often the dinette table mounts on a pedestal that can be removed. The table top then fits in front of the settee creating a much larger

platform for cushions.

Some part of the cabin sole should lift up, giving access to the bilge. Large hexagonal nuts on threaded bolts may be visible in the bilge. These keel bolts and nuts fasten the keel onto the boat.

A bilge pump, float switch and manual bilge pump intake hose sit in a dry bilge.

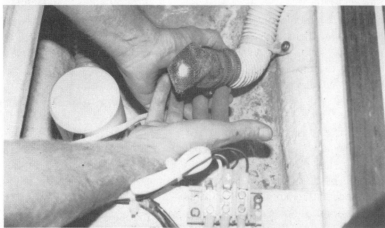

A screen on the intake hose keeps debris from fouling the bilge pump valves.

BILGE PUMPS

Water anywhere in the boat eventually flows to the bilge. The bilge pump draws water from the bilge and discharges it through the hull somewhere above the waterline. An automatic bilge pump consists of an electric pump and a float switch. Most systems use a waterproof pump which can sit in the bilge and be completely covered by water without danger. The float switch is also in the bilge. When the water level rises, the floating section of the switch rises and triggers the pump. It runs until the water level (and the float) drops far enough for the switch to turn the pump off.

Manual bilge pumps are necessary in case the automatic mechanism malfunctions. This system consists of the pump, discussed in Section I, the pick-up or intake hose and a strainer. Some sort of screen, a strainer, should be mounted at the very end of the hose to keep bilge debris from entering the pump and fouling its valves.

GALLEY

The galley or kitchen area has one thing in common with the head. Both pack a lot of utility into a very small space. The modern cruising sailboat falls short of offering all the comforts of home but not by much. Designers have done a commendable job of ensuring that the crew's important needs are satisfied. A broiler may double as a toaster or the cook may need re-training on a manual can opener, but most things culinary are possible with a little imagination. A detailed exploration of the galley and its components awaits in Section III. Meanwhile, familiarize yourself with the galley and its major components.

The ice box or refrigerator lies beneath the cut-out section of the counter top. Lift the lid using the lifting handle or ring pull. Notice the limited space. Also look for cold plates— metal refrigeration elements. If they are present the boat is equipped with mechanical refrigeration. If not, only ice keeps food cold and you must plan your passages accordingly.

The galley stove on this size boat usually has three burners on top and an oven/broiler. It looks small but it provides a surprisingly efficient cooking source. Most are mounted in gimbals that allow the stove top to remain horizontal when the boat heels. Galley stoves may use gas (either Compressed Natural Gas, CNG or Liquified Petroleum Gas, LPG or Propane) or alcohol as a fuel. Inspect all of the vertical surfaces in the galley area for a solenoid switch. The electrical switch regulates the source of LPG or CNG on boats that use these fuels. Specific instructions come later in Section III.

By now you have become expert at locating through-hulls. Trace the piping connected to the galley sink to find the through-hulls. In addition to the sink drain, the ice box has a drain which might route through a foot or hand pump.

The only really new thing here might be the intake line for a salt water pump. A very practical addition to the galley, this pump draws in seawater for use in cleaning, mostly dishes. It aids water conservation by reserving fresh water for rinsing

only. Seawater can also be used in cooking food which is sealed in plastic or capable of being rinsed afterward. Look for a small diameter nozzle or tube which rises from the counter top beside the sink and bends to point into the sink. It has no faucet but operates from a foot pump near the galley sole or a hand pump on the nozzle.

WATER CONSERVATION

The entire crew must be briefed on many subjects before any voyage. Make water conservation a high priority at briefing time.   The tank or tanks hold a limited supply; when they are empty that's the end of your water. Instruct your crew that water should never be left running. They should wash from a basin and wash dishes using a sink partly filled with water. Turn the faucet on only to rinse. Showers consist of rinsing, lathering with the water off, then rinsing again.

Dehydration can sneak up on sailors due to sea sickness or the body's increased need to perspire. Fluids should be replaced to avoid the clouded judgement, reduced initiative and costly mistakes associated with dehydration. The skipper should make sure that the crew stays well hydrated. Each crew member will need between a quart and a gallon per day just for survival.   Add two to five gallons for cooking and personal hygiene. Bodily water needs will be met from a variety of sources that include soda or juice. Some crew members may never actually drink a glass of water. A smart skipper watches his water supply the same way he watches the weather. Check it occasionally and be alert for any conditions which might cause it to change dramatically, sush as leaks.

The tanks on a boat may not be the best source of drinking water. The water may sit for months at a time and become stagnant and possibly unhealthy. Most marine stores sell additives which make the tank water more palatable. Draining the tanks, flushing and refilling them before departing also freshens the water supply. Alternatively, plan to carry jugs of water reserved for drinking.

Some fresh water tanks have valves to regulate water flowing from individual tanks into the system.

THE NAVIGATION STATION

If a sailboat had a brain it would be the navigation station. Both AC and DC electrical systems are usually controlled from here. Most navigation and communication electronics are located in this area. Charts and navigation tools are stored in the chart table. If you intend to do any serious cruising you should get comfortable in the navigation station as soon as possible. And if your interests lie in the ancient art of navigation, it will be the source of some wonderfully gratifying experiences.

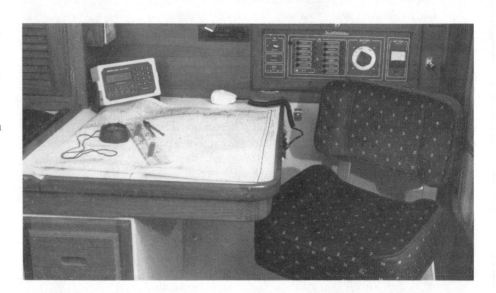

THE AC ELECTRICAL SYSTEM

You have already discovered the shore power cable and learned how to connect and remove it. With it attached and with the dock breaker on, power goes to the AC electrical panels in the nav station. It will be labeled AC or Shore Power.

A master switch on the panel sends power to the other switches. "On" and "off" positions should be clearly printed near the switch and a small indicator light may illuminate when the switch is on. Remember to turn the master switch off before removing the shore power cable. All switches on a modern cruising sailboat are circuit breakers and will trip off automatically in case there is

This AC panel has only two breakers, one master and one for the water heater.

an overload or a short circuit. The other switches usually operate the Battery Charger, Wall Outlets, Refrigeration and Hot Water.

Most boat owners leave the battery charger on whenever they leave the boat. It senses when the battery needs a boost and directs current to it at those times. The charger may be found under a settee or in the engine compartment. It needs ventilation. Although designed to supply the battery only with the power it needs, chargers have been known to overcharge batteries. Monitor the battery charge and electrolyte level in the battery regularly.

The wall outlets might have one switch for the whole boat, one for each side of the boat or one for each cabin. They accommodate anything which would run on electricity at home. Lights, fans, power tools and even a hair dryer (which will be good news if the crew includes teenage girls) can operate as long as the AC system has power.

Refrigeration can operate from AC, DC or battery power, an inverter or a compressor on the engine. It gets complicated when two or more of these systems are installed on the same boat. AC refrigeration offers a great opportunity to bring the temperature down on the cooling plates while dockside without running the engine or draining the battery. The refrigerator should be turned off, left free of perishables and with the lid open when the boat sits locked up at the dock. Turn it on as soon as possible if it has AC, a battery charger or the engine has been started. You can increase your perishables' life span by cooling the box down several hours before you prepare to shove off.

Hot water heaters appear on boats of 30 feet and larger. They usually heat fresh water using both a heat exchanger from the engine and electricity. The AC switch sends current to the heater. An internal thermostat turns off the heating element when the tank water has become sufficiently hot. Avoid the possibility of mishaps by leaving the switch off unless someone is aboard the boat.

THE DC ELECTRICAL SYSTEM

The DC system or "house system" draws its power from batteries. If you have not already located them, start looking under the remaining settee cushions and in and around the engine and bilge compartments. The batteries may be standard car batteries or larger marine storage batteries. The boat may also have "banks" of two or more batteries connected together. A separate battery for the anchor windlass and/or for starting the engine is not uncommon. Your challenge is to determine which batteries serve what purpose. Also, determine if the battery caps are removable to allow adding water or if they are "closed cell" batteries which cannot be filled. Use a light, if necessary, to see that the water level is up to the ring below the filler cap. If not, fill it the rest of the way with distilled water. Don't get any liquid from the battery on your skin or clothes. It will irritate the skin and burn holes in cloth.

The battery switch, which you located in Section I, routes the power from the main batteries or battery banks to all the things on board which use 12 volt DC current. In the previous section you switched from "Off" to "Both" or "All" to get battery power to the starter. A second look at the switch reveals two other settings, "1" and "2". When one of these settings is selected, power is drawn exclusively from that battery.

Unless someone has been kind enough to label the batteries, it will be difficult to determine which is 1 and which is 2. Carefully disconnect the cable from one of the positive terminals. The positive side will have a + carved into the top of the terminal or printed on the battery itself. With lights or the radio on, switch between "1" and "2" and figure out which one is not working. Once you have checked the water level and determined which is which, put everything back together.

Batteries must be held in place with a strong bracket or strap, even if they seem secure in a confined space. Otherwise, they could become airborne in rough weather.

Power flows from the batteries, to the battery switch and then to the main breaker on the DC panel. The panel will have a list showing the circuit activated by each of the switches. Make a habit of using the panel often. Leave everything off unless it is being used. Go to the panel and activate a circuit for use; return to the panel and turn it off after you have finished. This applies to water pressure, lights, electronics and anything else that has a switch. An automatic bilge pump might have on, off and auto settings. Leave it in auto. Make sure you know what each switch controls and how it works. <u>Check each one before shoving off.</u> Here are some typical switches and their functions.

Use hot water sparingly. The tank capacity is usually a fraction of what a home unit will hold.

Running Lights: A red light on the port bow, a green light on the starboard bow and a white light on the stern that allow you to be seen at night. They should be on when underway between sunset and sunrise and during other periods of reduced visibility.

Tricolor Light: A single light located at the top of the mast and showing the same arcs and colors as the running lights. Use it only under sail.

Bow Light : Also called Steaming Light, it is a white light usually half way up the mast, which faces forward. It indicates that the boat is under power.

Mast of Anchor Light: A white light at the top of the mast which can be seen from all directions. It should be illuminated when anchored at night in anything but a designated anchorage.

Cabin Lights: This switch controls all lights throughout the cabin. It must be on before their individual switches will function. Turn the panel switch off during daylight hours.

Water Pressure: This switch controls the pump which pressurizes the fresh water system. The pressure activated, automatic shut off in the system will keep the pump from running constantly. Leave it off and avoid a constant on and off cycle caused by slight pressure drops. The switch also keeps the pump from dumping your water supply in the bilge if a leak occurs in a line.

Macerator Pump: An electric pump installed on some boats to pump the contents of the holding tank overboard. Refer to the MARINE HEAD section for specific directions on its use.

Sump Pump: This supplies power to the switch for emptying drain water from the shower.

Radio: This switch usually controls power to an AM/FM radio, sometimes labeled "Stereo", but it may also supply the VHF.

Instruments: This switch could control many things but the depthsounder and knotmeter usually get power from this switch. It may also send power to the binnacle compass light.

Spare: Anything that did not get turned on by the other switches could be operated by a switch labeled spare.

VHF RADIO

VHF stands for very high frequency and it defines a set of radio frequencies (156-163MHz) which are assigned to marine communications. A VHF radio is tuned internally to these frequencies and it cannot be operated on different frequencies such as a short wave, amateur or CB. Marine VHF radio uses frequency - modulation (FM) signals, like those used in the FM stereo broadcast band. It is often referred to as VHF/FM.

The VHF is considered a radio station by the Federal Communications Commission. The station must be licensed and operated by a licensed individual. A marine electronics dealer or the nearest FCC office can supply you with applications for the appropriate licenses. The application process is relatively painless and takes only a few minutes.The major components of a VHF take many forms but the functions are the same. Look for the following after turning on the Radio/VHF switch on the DC panel.

On/off switch: Usually a knob or a push button, it should cause the dial to light up.

Volume adjustment: A knob or button which adjusts volume of the receiver speaker.

Channel selector: Another push button or dial with a light or digital display to illuminate the channel selected. Find it and determine which channels your radio is capable of receiving. It will vary.

Squelch: This device controls the receiver output. Adjust it by turning it down far enough to create static, then turn it back up until the static disappears. Broadcast messages will break through the silence without forcing you to listen to the aggravating static.

High/Low Switch: It has two settings and may also be labeled "1W" and

"25W". The W stands for watts and it denotes the power output of the radio. The low or 1watt setting is for calling a station which is close to you, perhaps within a mile. The high or 25 watt setting is for longer distances.

Microphone: Follow the curly cord and find the microphone. Hold it a few inches from your mouth when speaking. Pressing the button on the side will cut off the receiver and activate the transmitter. Release the button to hear a reply to your call. Calling ship to ship and ship to shore is discussed in Section III.

WEATHER RADIO

The National Oceanographic and Atmospheric Administration (NOAA) operates an impressive system of radio stations throughout the country. These stations broadcast weather information 24 hours a day. They are updated periodically and the broadcasts will mention when the current information was gathered. Listen for recorded information on weather channels often labeled "W1" or "WX1". There may also be as many as ten channels in the radio receiver but currently (1991) only three are in use.

NOAA radio forecasts are prepared for the wide area covered by the station. As a result, the information is not always accurate for a specific locality and sailors have heard about a perilous weather condition only after they have survived it. Despite its shortcomings, listening to NOAA radio should be as much a part of your pre-sail routine as opening the companionway hatch and uncovering the mainsail. Many lives have been saved by the information supplied by this valuable service. Many a sailor beleaguered by deteriorating weather has wished he had taken a moment to listen to NOAA radio regularly, both before and during his voyage.

The rest of the navigation station is self explanatory. Most chart tables lift on hinges. The compartment below is ideal for storing navigation equipment and important items such as registration papers and keys. Drawers are usually built into the woodwork below the chart table.

THE ENGINE

Your previous study of the engine section answered a few important questions. Now roll up your sleeves and prepare to find out what makes this beast tick. Convenience, safety and punctuality all benefit from your knowledge of the inboard auxiliary engine. Section V, Emergencies &Trouble Shooting, will explain how to perform simple repairs on serviceable engine parts. The following information explains how the engine and its components work.

GENERAL INSPECTION

You will find the engine somewhere aft of the bilge and forward of the rudder post. The ladder from the cabin to the cockpit is a good place to start. Opening clasps and latches in this area should give access to the engine.

Once the enclosure has been removed, identify the major components in the drive train. The engine and transmission bolt together. One end of the propellor shaft attaches to a coupling on the transmission. The other end disappears into a metal fitting, perhaps with some rubber mounted around it, called the stuffing box. Find the through-hull which brings raw sea water into the cooling system and make sure the valve is open.

The propellor shaft (left) turns inside the stuffing box.

GAS OR DIESEL

Reliability and safety have made small diesel engines the exclusive choice among today's sailboat manufacturers. Older boats may have either gas or diesel engines. A quick glance will disclose your engine's fuel requirement. A rectangular, sheet metal valve cover sits on top of most engines. It may have a removable cap for adding oil. Tap it and it sounds hollow. Below the cover, on one side, you will find either a set of heavy flexible wires leading to spark plugs or rigid metal tubing connected to fuel injectors. Spark plugs ignite gasoline; injectors feed diesel. An engine cannot have both. If you know your way around car engines you will recognize a distributor cap. Its wires conduct electrical impulses to spark plugs and they are found only on gas engines. Use this as a means of double checking.

OIL

The machinery inside the engine block needs oil for lubrication just like a car. Find the dip stick somewhere on the engine block. Check the oil by removing the dip stick, wiping it clean, re-inserting it all the way and taking it out again. The oil level on the stick indicates the amount in the engine. Most dip sticks have lines engraved on them to indicate the proper range of oil level. The distance between two lines usually represents one quart. Fill to the top line. Add oil when necessary by opening the filler and carefully pouring in the oil. If the filler is not located on the metal valve cover it will be somewhere else accessible on the top of the engine.

Another filler for engine coolant may be located nearby. Dipping a finger into either filler should bring out enough residue to determine which one you have opened. Make sure the engine is cool to the touch before inserting a finger. Eliminate any doubts about the identity of the filler before adding oil or coolant. Estimate the amount needed, add it and check the level again. Do not overfill. Keep a rag handy to wipe up spills.

ENGINE COOLING

Thousands of controlled explosions inside the engine's cylinders enable the engine to start and run. Each explosion generates intense heat. The cooling system ensures that the engine remains at a reasonable temperature. Without cooling, the engine and its components would melt, burn or seize.

THE CLOSED SYSTEM

An automobile engine uses a radiator and a fan for cooling. Cooling liquid circulates through the engine block where it absorbs the heat of engine combustion. The hot water then passes through coils within the radiator. A high speed fan draws air over the coils to cool the water inside before it returns to the engine block to absorb more combustion heat. The coolant expands when it is heated. The entire system inside the engine, radiator and hoses is sealed and will resist the pressure of water expansion. A cap on the radiator releases excess pressure if the temperature rises above an acceptable level. We call this overheating, and on hot summer days our nation's highways are littered with its victims.

Inboard, auxiliary engines have the same need for cooling but they satisfy that need in a somewhat different way. The reservoir of liquid which pumps through the engine is called the closed system. Locate the filler cap which should be on top of a small cast iron tank. If the engine is cool to the touch, remove the cap and check the fluid level. (Never open the cap on a hot engine. The sudden release could blow dangerous boiling water and steam out through the cap.) The fluid level should be within an inch of the top. If not, you may replace the missing coolant with tap water. It will mix with the brightly colored coolant. Running the engine at idle for a moment may draw the level down by releasing trapped air bubbles. If so, top it off again and make sure the cap is secure before you cover up the engine.

A rubber belt or belts run over a series of pulleys somewhere on the front of the engine. One pulley turns the water pump, an oddly shaped cast iron housing with two thick hoses attached. The pump circulates water through the closed system.

RAW WATER SYSTEM

You have already located the through-hull for the engine's sea water. Follow the hose toward the engine. Find a raw water strainer attached somewhere along the hose. The strainer is frequently inside a glass bowl. It prevents debris from traveling further into the system. Debris on the strainer can restrict the flow of water. Locate the fastening devices, often knobs, nuts or wing nuts, which hold the bowl in place.

Continue following the hose. It enters a small, metal housing which has another hose attached. This is the raw water pump which draws the seawater in and forces it through the system. Continue following the hose out of the raw water pump and it will lead to a cast iron tank known as the heat exchanger. Inside, the two cooling systems meet but only through the protection of a series of metal coils, like the car radiator. Their liquids never mix. The cool ocean water passes over the coils cooling the fluid from the closed system which continues pumping through the engine. The raw water may go on to cool engine oil and transmission fluid before it flows to a pot-like "water lift" muffler and then is pushed out the exhaust line at the stern with the engine exhaust gases.

FUEL SYSTEM

Your exploration of the spaces below various berths and settees may have uncovered the fuel tank. If not, continue looking in the engine area and under aft berths. Follow the line from the deck filler if necessary. Locate all lines in and out of the tank. The large filler hose runs from the deck filler to the tank. The remaining smaller hoses are the fuel line and the vent. A return line may also bring unused fuel back from the injectors. The fuel line leads off in the direction of the engine while the vent attaches to a fitting somewhere high on the hull.

Follow the line and locate the shut-off, a valve somewhere between the tank and the engine. Most valves have a single operating lever and they work just like a seacock. The valve is open when the lever points parallel to the line and closed when it runs perpendicular. Leave the fuel line open unless fuel flow must be stopped for repairs.

The system may run the fuel through a fuel separator on its way to the engine. Most separators have a filter element, called a primary filter, on the top. The separator is a glass reservoir where water and fine sediment can settle out of the fuel. Water and sediment look different from fuel in color and clarity when seen through the bowl. A valve at the bottom of the bowl lets you release the water and sediment.

If the primary filter is not attached to the separator, it will be nearby in the fuel line. A secondary fuel filter is also a key element in the harmonious operation of your engine. It may take on a variety of forms. One common variety resembles the raw water strainer because a bowl or canister is suspended from a fitting along the fuel line. The bowl is smaller than the one on the strainer and it may not be clear. The working part of the filter is a paper element which fits inside the bowl. The filter element may be removable or the bowl and element may get replaced as one unit.

FUEL PUMP

The fuel pump maintains a steady flow of fuel to the engine. Some engines use an electric pump, frequently mounted close to the fuel tank. Most diesels use a mechanical pump mounted on the engine block. It may be necessary to see around corners and fit into small places to follow the fuel line from the tank to the engine. Trying to locate fuel filters often leaves you no choice.

Many fuel pumps have a lever or lift pump to draw fuel from the tank by hand. We will work with the lift pump in Section V. If you have plenty of light and a clear view, the lift pump may be visible. If not, gently trace the contour of the pump with your hand. A little pressure here and there should reveal a part of the mechanism which moves. It is the manual lift pump. Give it a few strokes to get the feel of how it works.

INJECTOR SYSTEM

Diesel engines mix fuel and air in their cylinders which, under great pressure, heats to the point of combustion driving the pistons down and turning the crankshaft. The air/fuel mixture is probably the most delicate part of the whole process.

INJECTOR PUMP

After the fuel has left the tank, had any water removed and passed through the filter, the fuel pump delivers it to the injector pump. This pump looks very much like other angular pieces of metal attached to the engine block. Follow the fuel line out of the fuel pump and it will eventually go into the injector pump. The line into the injector pump may be metal or rubber but the line out will always be metal. The injector pump discharges fuel under hundreds of pounds of pressure and only metal lines can contain the force.

INJECTORS

Fuel from the injector pump moves through the metal line to the injectors. The injectors atomize the fuel, turning it into a super-fine mist so that when it mixes with air the combination is nearly a vapor. Each injector has a fitting where the line from the injector pump attaches. The other line attached to each injector is the return. It may be a smaller diameter line which connects all of the injectors. The return directs surplus fuel back to the fuel system when the injector pump supplies more than the engine requires.

A primary diesel fuel filter element and fuel separator are often found in one unit.

(A) fuel pump (the lift pump is not visible),
(B) secondary fuel filter,
(C) injector pump,
(D) high pressure injector lines

TRANSMISSION

The transmission, a metal casing considerably smaller than the engine, usually protrudes from the aft end of the engine and has fins molded into it for cooling. Locate the filler, a threaded cap that bolts into the transmission casing. It may have a hex nut or some other configuration on the top to facilitate its removal with a wrench or pliers. Also find the dip stick. Some transmissions have the dip stick attached to the plug for the filler. Remove the plug and the dip stick appears. Others may have no dip stick at all. Check the fluid level by putting something like a pencil into the hole. Use your finger if you have a rag nearby.

Use only the type of fluid recommended for your particular transmission. It will be stamped on the filler plug or somewhere on the transmission. Also look for the gear lever. It can be operated from the transmission in the event of cable failure.

Transmission filler and dip stick are one piece on this boat. Shift lever (A) and propeller shaft and coupling (left) are also visible.

ELECTRICAL SYSTEM

You already found the belt that runs the water pump. Look in the same area for an alternator, a slotted metal housing with two or more wires connected to it. The alternator creates electricity when the belt turns it at high speed. It charges the batteries and runs the house electrical system. Check the belt, possibly the same one that drives the water pump, for tension and wear. It should move no more than 3/4 of an inch when you pull it out from its perimeter. See Section V for details on adjusting the belt.

The starter motor can be found somewhere near the transmission. Recognize it by its long, cylindrical metal housing. Either on the starter or nearby, sits the solenoid switch. It sends electrical power to the starter when the key or start button is activated. Also, look for the heavy cable that brings power to the solenoid and another from the solenoid to the starter.

(A) Alternator and (B) water pump often run off the same belt.

COCKPIT DRAINS

You identified the scuppers for the cockpit drains on deck. You should be able to see where they lead from the engine compartment. If they empty below the water line they will lead to a through-hull or through-hulls. Remember their location and the type of valve at the through-hull. They remain open unless it becomes necessary to seal the hull in an emergency.

THE AFT CABIN

The boat may have an aft cabin. If so, your exploring skills will come in handy once again. If not, locate the following systems and equipment beneath the cockpit and in the cockpit lockers and lazarette.

Trace the steering mechanism. You found the rudder post extension in Section I. The emergency tiller on some cruising boats must be operated from inside the aft cabin. The helmsman stands hunched over with his or her head sticking up through the hatch cover.

Emergency tillers tend to be somewhat difficult to operate. Either they are short with little leverage or they stand only inches above the cockpit sole so you have to lean over them to steer. Proper care of the steering mechanism can reduce the possibility of using the emergency tiller. Loose cables can slip off sheaves. Turnbuckles and threaded cable ends are a common means of adjustment. When two nuts are present on the same cable end, the outside nut is a locking device and the inside nut is an adjustment. Hold the adjusting nut in place with a wrench. Loosen the locking nut, then adjust the cable length with the other nut and screw the locking nut tightly against it.

Everything else in the aft cabin should be familiar. Some of the tanks and plumbing described in the previous material may be located there. An aft head might have its own holding tank, macerator, "Y" valve and overboard discharge.

FUEL PLANNING

Space travelers in science fiction always seem to have an unlimited supply of everything necessary to sustain their lives and their mission. Perhaps sailors are doomed by the antiquated nature of their vessels or maybe there is too much fiction in the space traveler tales. Either way, sailors do not enjoy the luxury of any unlimited commodity. Even the supply of salt water gets a little thin close to shore.

Aside from fresh water and ice, fuel is one of the most important commodities in planning your voyage. Just making sure the tanks are full does not constitute proper planning. There are other important details you should know.

FUEL CAPACITY

How much fuel will the tanks hold? Owner's manuals and manufacturer's printed material may answer this question. Older boats may not have documentation on board. The manufacturer or dealer might provide an answer, or ask the owner of a sister ship. The last resort, draining the tank and refilling it, is dangerous and cumbersome. Avoid it if at all possible.

FUEL CONSUMPTION

The owner's information should include the amount of fuel the engine requires at various speeds. It usually consists of a graph showing engine speed (RPM) on one axis and fuel consumption (Gallons per Hour or GPH) on the other. It may also contain a recommendation for maximum RPM. On this graph you would find a speed range where fuel consumption shoots up dramatically in relation to a small increase in RPM. Keep the engine below this speed for maximum efficiency.

A fuel log is a diary which provides you with fuel consumption information. Begin with a full tank. Record the amount of engine use time. Assume that most of the time spent motoring is at cruising RPMs. Note the amount of fuel at your next fill-up, then divide the number of gallons by the number of hours.

Example:

$$\begin{array}{r} 17 \text{ Gallons} \\ \div\ \ 38 \text{ Hours} \\ \hline =\ \ .447 \text{ Gallons/Hr} \end{array}$$

This figure could be rounded off at 1/2 GPH. To be safe, always round off to a higher number, never to a lower number. Engine RPMs will vary during your logged engine time but recording an estimated average RPM will further refine your fuel consumption estimates.

Most boats manufactured recently have fuel gauges. They are susceptible to salt water corrosion and may not last beyond a few years. Some tanks have fillers or inspection caps directly above the tank. They can be checked by "dipping" or lowering a stick to the bottom of the tank like an oil dip stick. Keeping a log and topping off the tank yield better results.

RANGE UNDER POWER

Range refers to the distance a boat can travel under power with the amount of fuel it can store. Sailboats are not as limited by fuel capacity as are power boats. A power boat with a range of 1500 miles would never embark on the 2400 mile trip from Hawaii to the mainland but a sailboat with similar range would be quite comfortable with the same trip. In fact, the skipper of the sailboat would expect to sail more than 900 miles and have plenty of fuel to spare. Sailors may not be as restricted by their range under power but they should be equally conscious of it.

You need to know one additional variable before you can compute range: the boat's speed at comfortable cruising RPM. Experiment with the RPM setting discussed earlier and record the speed as accurately as possible. Compare knotmeter readings to navigational plots and match your data with that obtained by other boats on the same course and speed.

Once you have determined speed, plug it into this equation.

$$\begin{array}{rl} & \text{Speed (In knots)} \\ \div & \text{Consumption} \\ \hline = & \text{NMPG (Nautical Miles/Gallon)} \\ & \text{(in one hour)} \end{array}$$

$$\begin{array}{rl} & \text{NMPG} \\ \times & \text{Fuel Capacity} \\ \hline = & \text{Range in Nautical Miles} \end{array}$$

As the level of fuel in the tanks falls, the chances of drawing air through the fuel line increase. The fuel at the bottom of the tank contains more sediment and contaminants. Air or dirt in the fuel represent the diesel engine's most common reasons for quitting. Never plan to burn all the fuel in the tank.

Compute your boat's range based on a fuel capacity about 1/8 less than what the tank will hold. That means 1/8th tank will remain even when you have depleted the supply computed in your range equation. This method understates your range but it will ensure that you can motor the entire distance without drawing air or sediment through the fuel lines.

REDUCED RANGE

Once you have determined your boat's range under power, you may plan the motoring portion of your voyage. How much motoring time are you likely to need? Use past experience or advice from experienced sailors to come up with an estimate. There are some factors other than fuel and fuel consumption which will affect your range under power. Consider them carefully when estimating your range and use them to revise your range estimates while underway.

Condition of the hull: Marine life grows constantly on the hull of any boat. A diver can clean the hull and reduce its resistance as it moves through the water. A clean hull is a prerequisite for any long passage.

Weight: Full water and fuel tanks and a load of people, provisions and gear can significantly increase a boat's total weight. It takes more power to move added weight and your RPM, fuel consumption and speed could all be affected adversely.

Wind: Wind from ahead will slow your progress, wind from astern will increase your speed.

Waves and swells: Short, choppy waves are most often accompanied by wind and contribute to its overall effect. Swells cause the boat to travel up and down hills. The distance traveled over the hills is further than the straight line distance over the ground thereby reducing your range.

You will discover that many of the skills necessary to master the art of navigation are nothing more than best estimates. More information and a greater understanding of the governing conditions will make navigating more pleasurable and precise.

SECURING TO A DOCK

The chafing effect of wind and current on dock lines has already been mentioned. You must also take precautions to anticipate the effects of rising and falling tides. Tidal ranges of five feet or more are not uncommon in coastal regions of the United States. A boat tied securely to a dock at high tide could find itself in trouble when the water level drops five feet. Dock lines, deck hardware and dock cleats are all at risk. Failure of any of these items could cause additional damage to the boat.

Synthetic fiber dock lines, like so many materials we take for granted, have evolved into a reliable, high quality hybrid of their coarse natural fiber ancestors. With the ends whipped and chafing prevented, today's lines could outlast the boat or its owner. We can use a line which stretches to our advantage in areas of high tidal range. Three strand laid nylon line will stretch up to 25% under load , but will return to its original length when the load has been removed.

Increasing the length of a dock line increases its stretching capability. Notice the diagram below. Spring lines extend nearly the length of the boat. Bow and stern lines are led at angles which increase their length while holding the boat securely to the dock.

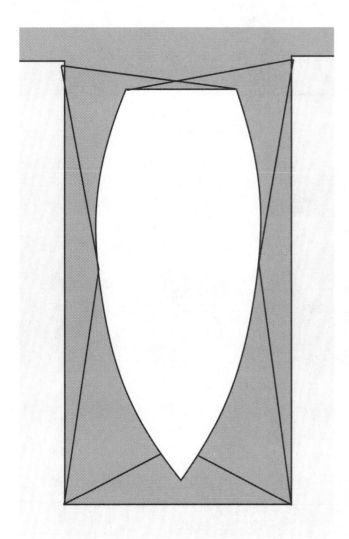

1. _____are valves that allow water to pass in and out of the hull.

2. _____ are sensors which feed information to the knotmeter and depthsounder.

3. The_____pumps waste water from the shower overboard.

4. Beyond_____miles from the coast we may operate our _____to pump out the contents of the holding tank.

5. The two common gases used for cooking aboard pleasure boats are_____ and _____.

6. Each crew member needs between a_____and a_____of water per day just for survival.

7. The_____radio allows us to communicate between boats and from boat to shore.

8. The _____separates debris from cooling sea water.

9. Water and sediment are eliminated from fuel by a _____.

10. A boat's_____is the distance it can travel with the amount of fuel it can store.

Circle the correct true or false answers below

11. True or false? Turn a seacock parallel to its fitting to stop the flow of water.

12. True or false? Pump the head with the intake valve closed to clear water from the bowl after using the head.

13. True or false? Manual bilge pumps are not necessary when automatic bilge pumps are installed.

14. True or false? Diesel engines are equipped with distributor caps.

15. True or false? Steering cables are adjustable and should be checked periodically for tension.

16. True or false? Your boat has 10 gallons of fuel on board and it burns 1/2 gallon/hr at a cruising speed of 5.5 knots. You intend to keep 3 gallons of fuel in reserve. Will you be able to motor to your home port which is 60 miles away?

SAILING SKILLS

All of the tasks necessary to safely and confidently move the boat from one location to another are called Sailing Skills. Sailing may only be a small part of some voyages. Engine and plumbing repairs, navigation, weather forecasting and other important non-sail related chores may take up most of your time. You remain in control as long as the demands of the situation do not exceed your acquired skills. A diversity of skills is important as a result.

CHECKLIST FOR GETTING UNDERWAY

With the knowledge gained from getting acquainted with the boat above deck in Section I and below deck in Section II comes a responsibility. From now on, prior to leaving the slip, you and your crew must inspect each item necessary for the smooth operation of the vessel. Make these checks each time you prepare to get underway regardless of whether you are leaving home port or an overnight anchorage. Eliminate the possibility of forgetting important items by following the printed list in Appendix C.

KNOTS

The basic knots sailors learn prior to undertaking serious cruising will meet the demands of most situations. You should be an old salt when it comes to tying a square knot, Bowline, clove hitch, figure 8, overhand knot and two half hitches. Special needs, however, call for specialized knots. An inquisitive sailor should always take the time to learn a new knot. It may be the next knot you need.

ROLLING HITCH

The diagram shows that the Rolling Hitch resembles a Clove Hitch. It goes together like a Clove Hitch except for the addition of an extra turn in the first part of the hitch. The Rolling Hitch is a more secure version of the Clove Hitch. The Rolling Hitch adds greater lateral holding power when the strain on the hitch is not perpendicular. Tie the rolling hitch so that the lateral pull is away from the final half hitch turn. (figure D)

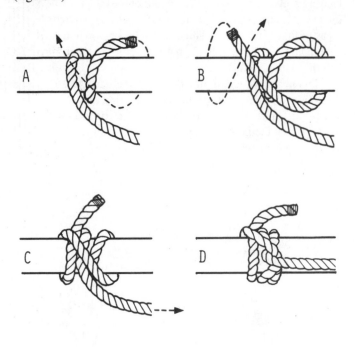

TRUCKER'S HITCH

The Trucker's Hitch comes in handy for cinching down a load, such as a dinghy on the foredeck. The knot's construction features a built-in 2:1 purchase. Notice that the loops created in Illustration B are held in place strictly by pressure from the load on the knot. That simplifies the chore of getting the knot untied despite the load created by the 2:1 purchase.

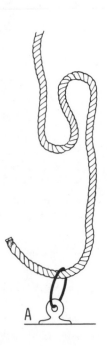

THE CHART

Maps are handy for finding our way along interstate highways or locating hidden treasure. The publications which supply information about our waterways are called Charts. Every sailor should take time to read and understand the information a nautical chart offers. You may not immediately know how to use the chart's data but you will know the right questions to ask when the time comes.

Coastal charts in the U. S. are distributed and maintained by NOAA, the same agency that brings us the continuous weather broadcasts on VHF radios. Many inland lakes, even big ones, have no government chart for boaters. Sailors in these areas should acquire a chart from any coastal area for familiarity and practice. The ASA offers an excellent Coastal Navigation home study course which includes practice charts. Look for the following important items on the chart.

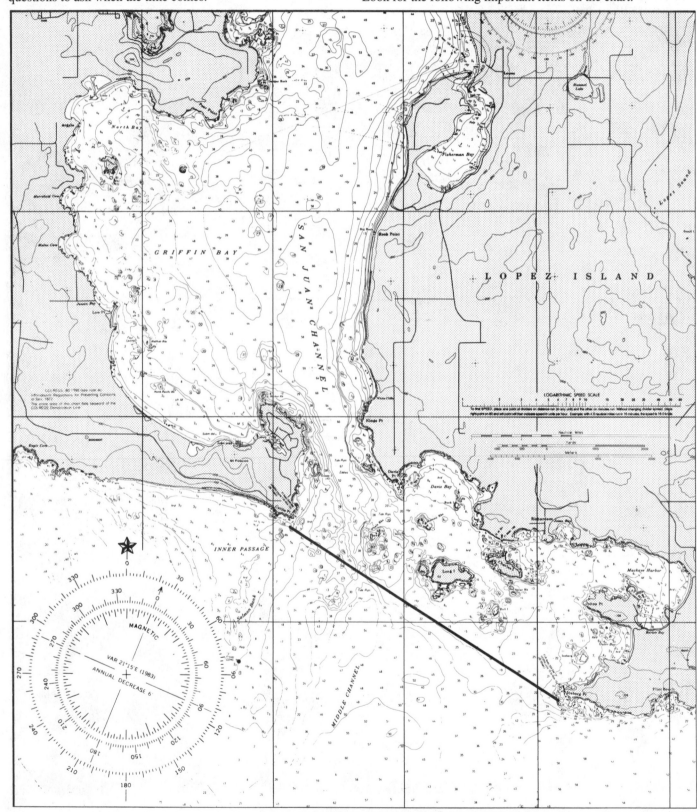

Longitude: The measurement of distance around the earth horizontally east -west. The Prime Meridian which runs north and south through Greenwich, England is "0". Positions west of this line are expressed as West Longitude; positions east are in East Longitude. East meets west at the International Date Line which runs through the Pacific Ocean roughly halfway around the earth from the Prime Meridian.

Latitude: The measurement of distance on the earth in a north - south direction. The equator is "0". Positions above the equator are said to be in North Latitude, those below are in South Latitude.

Degrees and Minutes: Both latitude and longitude are measured in degrees. Lines of latitude are evenly spaced from the north pole to the south pole. Lines of longitude are closer together near the poles than they are at the equator. Each degree is divided into 60 minutes. Minutes are divided into multiples of ten and labeled. For example, each of the ten equal divisions between 33°10' and 33°20' represents one minute of latitude. Minutes are further divided into fractions of ten using a decimal point on most charts. The longitude scale is similarly divided and labeled. For example, the latitude of the international airport at Los Angeles is written as: 33°57.2'N.

We use the latitude scale to measure distance on a chart because the lines are evenly spaced. One degree of latitude equals 60 nautical miles. One minute of latitude is one nautical mile. Always use the latitude scales located on the right and left sides of the chart to measure off distance.

Compass Rose: Most charts have more than one. It is a circle within a circle of tiny lines and numbers. The outer circle is the True Compass Rose and the "0" on the outer circle points to true north or the very top of the earth. The inner circle is the Magnetic Compass Rose and

"0" on this circle points to magnetic north, the direction a compass will indicate when pointing north.

Variation: The angular difference between true and magnetic north. It is written inside the compass rose and differs from region to region.

Chart symbols: Diagrams and abbreviated words on a chart give mariners information about their surroundings, such as shoreline features, bottom characteristics, lighthouses and buoy locations and hazardous wrecks.

Depth Soundings: Most of the water portion of the chart has numbers printed throughout. They indicate depth. The title block and the top and bottom margins state whether the chart uses "Soundings in Fathoms" or "Soundings in Feet". To conform to international standards, all charts will eventually shift to meter depth measurements. Charts marked "Soundings in Meters" are increasingly common. A fathom is six feet while a meter is 3.1 feet.

Chart No. 1: A NOAA publication which lists the chart symbols and their meanings.

The navigation information in this text is only a simple primer for the full treatment of the subject which you should study later.

PLOTTING TOOLS

Parallel rules and dividers, the two major navigation tools, have changed very little in the past few hundred years. While some useful new tools perform the same functions, students are well advised to learn the parallel rules and dividers first. Put them away in your sea bag if you prefer more modern plotting tools, but in time you will probably dig out your old tools and be glad you kept them handy.

Parallel Rules: Two straight edge rulers connected by pivoting arms which allow them to move a few inches apart. The two outside edges remain parallel. Try "walking" the rulers between lines of latitude. Line up one edge along the line on the chart and press it against the chart. Swing the other ruler in the direction of the other line. When the movable ruler is as far away from the stationary ruler as possible, press it solidly onto the chart table holding it and the chart in place. The other edge is now free to swing back up to meet it. Repeat the process until one of the edges reaches the designated line. You can walk all over the chart and both rulers will remain parallel to the original line as long as neither ruler slips. Always use the outside edges for drawing lines.

Dividers: The two arms on the dividers separate to measure and hold distance between two points.

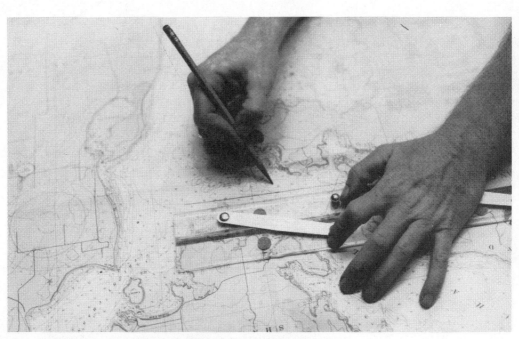

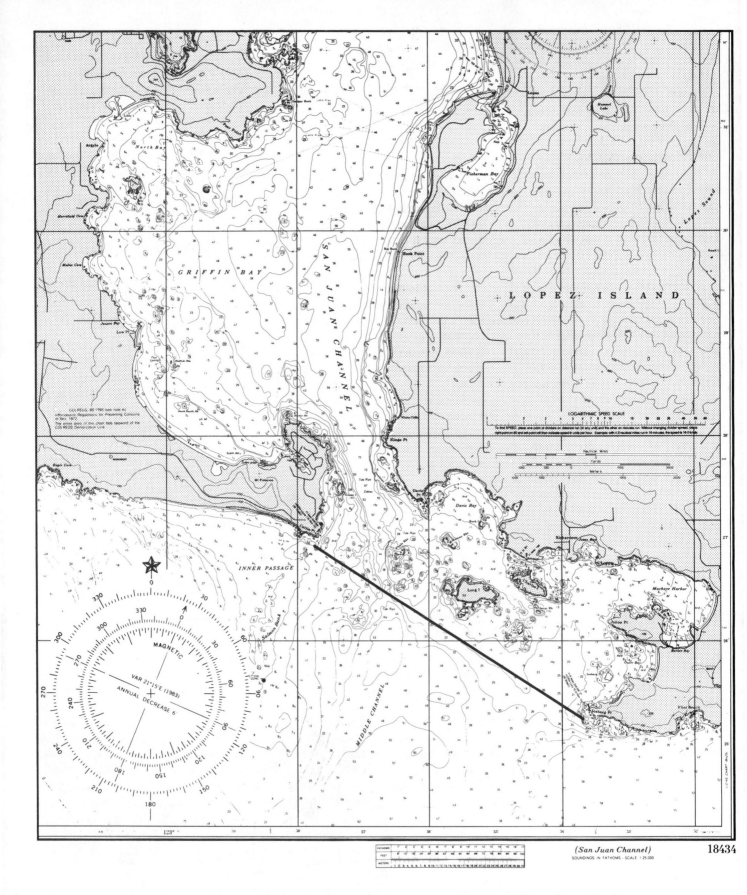

This "track" runs between two points of land over water depths which are sufficient for navigation.

LAYING OFF A COURSE

Spread out the chart of your cruising area. Find your point of origin and destination. Draw a pencil line or track between the two. Inspect this path to be sure it will keep you in depths much deeper than the boat's draft. If the line goes over land or shallow water, draw a series of lines which connect the two through deep water.

COMPASS COURSE

Open the chart so the track line and a compass rose are as close to the center of the chart table as possible. Place the parallel rules on the chart so one edge lines up along the track. Walk the parallel rules to the compass rose. Experimentation may uncover a starting position for the parallel rules which makes the trip to the compass rose easier. It may take a few tries to get it right.

Once you get to the compass rose, find the tiny cross in the middle of the rose and set up either outside edge of the parallel rules so it runs through the center. Think of the cross as the point of origin and follow the straight edge in the direction you will be traveling when you make your voyage. Make sure the straight edge has been positioned so it extends beyond the cross to pass over both true and magnetic compass roses. Make a note of the number where the edge passes over the magnetic compass rose. This will be your magnetic course. Above your course line near the point of origin, write "C" (the number from the magnetic compass rose) "M". For example C240M. This tells you the course to steer by magnetic compass on that leg of the voyage. If you know your cruising speed it should be recorded below the track line as follows: "S 5.5".

DISTANCE

Take the dividers and place one point on the starting position. Open the dividers and place the other point on the destination. Go to the latitude scale and read off the distance between the points. If the dividers cannot span the entire distance, open them slightly less than their full span. Find the latitude scale on either side of the chart. Set the dividers to a convenient distance - perhaps one, two or five miles. Make a note of this distance. Use the dividers to measure a series of steps of this distance along the line and add their total. Shorten the gap between divider points when the remaining distance is less than your original measurement. Add all of the distances. Fractions of a minute may be indicated on the individual minute markings or you may have to estimate. Be as precise as possible.

SPEED, TIME & DISTANCE

Speed in boating is expressed in nautical miles per hour or "knots". We are discussing speed; but we understand it in terms of miles, which are a measurement of distance, and hours, which are a measurement of time. Speed, time and distance are inseparable and if you know any two you can always find the third.

An easy way to remember the equation for speed, time and distance is to remember this address, 60 D STreet. That should be enough to bring back the equation 60D=ST, 60 X Distance =Speed X Time. Then just plug in the numbers you know and find the one you seek.

Basic algebra tells us this formula can also be expressed in the following forms to solve for whichever single variable may be missing.

$$D=ST/60$$
$$S=60D/T$$
$$T=60D/S$$

D=distance in nautical miles, S=speed in knots and T=time in minutes.

Look at the course we plotted earlier. You know the distance because we walked it off on the latitude scale and made a note of the total. For example, suppose the distance was 25 nautical miles. Our earlier exercises with the knotmeter indicated our approximate cruising speed. We'll use 5.5 knots for our example. We know S and D, so the equation above with the T by itself will work.

$$\frac{60D}{S}=T \quad \frac{60 \times 25}{5.5}=T \quad \frac{1500}{5.5}=T$$
$$272.7=T$$

There are a few important things to remember here. This time is in minutes. Divide by 60 to get the number of hours. In this case, 4 hours. Don't calculate a decimal fraction here. The remainder of 33 is the number of minutes left over after 4 hours have been extracted. The total time required to cover 25 nautical miles at 5.5 knots is 4 hours and 33 minutes.

The conditions which affected your estimate of the boat's range affect your speed, time and distance. So will other factors including current and leeway. These are discussed in navigation courses. For the moment, a basic understanding of the interrelation of these elements will suffice as a basis from which to build your navigation skills.

MANEUVERING UNDER POWER

Section I explored the forces which affect an inboard auxiliary equipped sailboat under power. The overall feel of a larger boat takes some adjustment time. It moves differently under power and has a different set of reflexes than a small boat. The following exercises and their explanations should guide you through the practice necessary to make the boat as predictable as the gusty winds and blue skies which follow a passing cold front.

GETTING THE BOAT MOVING

Find a practice spot which is open yet sheltered from wind, waves, traffic and other obstructions. Start with the boat idling in neutral with plenty of sea room ahead. Shift to forward. Add about 300 RPMs every minute until you reach the level described in the FUEL CONSUMPTION section. This will probably be between 2000 to 2500 RPMs. Add speed gradually to limit strain on the propulsion system.

Notice how long it takes for the boat to reach cruising speed. The knotmeter responds gradually every time the RPMs increase. Once the tachometer has reached its efficient maximum speed, the knotmeter may take another minute or more to reach cruising speed. Use this exercise to become aware of the larger boat's limitations when putting way on. The burst of speed needed to get out of a tricky situation may come slowly.

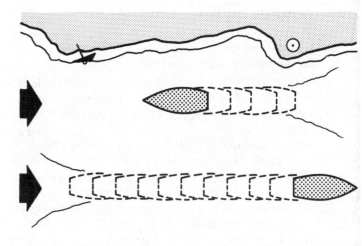

The wind (indicated by arrows) increases the speed of a boat traveling in the same direction (bottom) and decreases a boat's speed moving toward the wind direction (top).

STOPPING THE BOAT

Another, more profound characteristic of larger, heavier boats makes itself known when you take way off or slow the boat down. A boat must be nearly stopped before it comes into contact with anything. A one or one and a half knot collision with a sea wall or another boat can be a disaster.

From cruising speed, slow the engine to idle and put it into neutral. Notice the boat's location when you begin to glide and watch the knotmeter until it is well under one half knot. The distance you've traveled may come as a surprise.

Repeat the exercise, except this time shift from neutral into reverse and add a few hundred RPMs. Note the shorter stopping distance. Reverse is the boat's "brake" but shift or throttle mechanism failure could force you to do without it. Watching the boat come to a stop from a glide will allow you to plan for that possibility.

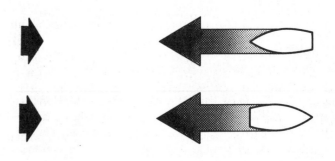

Motoring into the wind can keep the boat from moving over the ground.

STOPPING NEAR A MARKER

Bringing the bow of the boat up to a buoy, another boat or an object in the water may become necessary. There are two basic complications. Both your boat and the other object may be moving and the larger boat's length means the helmsman is further from the object.

You may be lucky enough to have chosen a wide fairway with an unobstructed buoy somewhere in the middle for motoring practice. If not, select a central location and set an anchor with a buoy attached to the line. Fenders make good buoys.

The object is to approach the buoy from downwind, upwind and with the wind across the beam. It is advisable to select a target spot a boat length or so beside the buoy rather than the buoy itself. Use the buoy only as a reference, especially if you are using a large, metal buoy. By staying at least a boat length away you won't get trapped if the wind catches the hull and you begin to drift.

You will soon discover that wind across the beam creates havoc for the helmsman. The boat will not come to rest for more than a moment. Fortunately, you will usually find that either a downwind or an upwind approach is possible.

Upwind approaches have the advantage of motoring in forward, a choice you learned to favor in the docking exercise. With little or no way on, the hull will drift rapidly away from the mark if the wind catches one side or the other.

Downwind the hull is less likely to present a broad surface to the wind but maneuverability in reverse could be very limited.

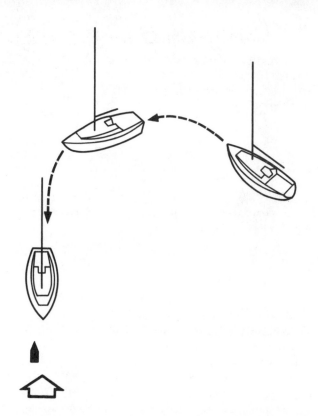

Approach a fixed marker from down wind whenever possible. Turn into the wind at least 2-3 boat lengths from your destination. This will allow you time to adjust your speed.

CIRCLES

With the boat stopped, turn the wheel from full left to full right or "stop to stop". Note how many revolutions the wheel turned. Half the total number of turns brings the rudder onto the centerline (amidships) and the boat would steer straight if it were making way. You may be able to confirm the rudder's position by looking over the stern or later under the hull from the dock. Mark the wheel's amidships position by wrapping tape at the top of the wheel. You may notice a turk's head knot marking this position on some boats.

Get the boat under way and increase speed to 2 or 3 knots. Ensuring you have adequate sea room, turn hard to one side. Make a few complete circles, then do the same in the other direction.

The main factor in a boat's turning radius is its keel. A short, fin keel allows the boat to turn in a smaller circle. A 1/2, 3/4 or full keel creates a larger circle. Knowing what to expect from your boat will help you judge when to make turns.

Some boats are manufactured with the propellor shaft slightly off center. The boat always turns in the same direction whenever the helm is left unattended with the wheel brake off. This can be a great safety feature if the only person on deck falls overboard.

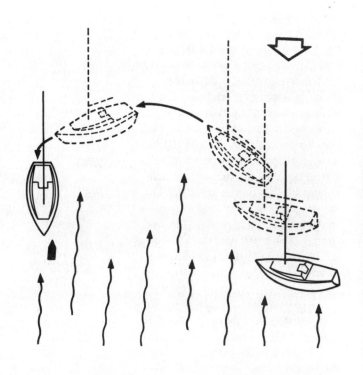

Wind and current may occur in different directions. Make a slow practice approach to the marker and determine what effect the prevailing forces will have on the boat.

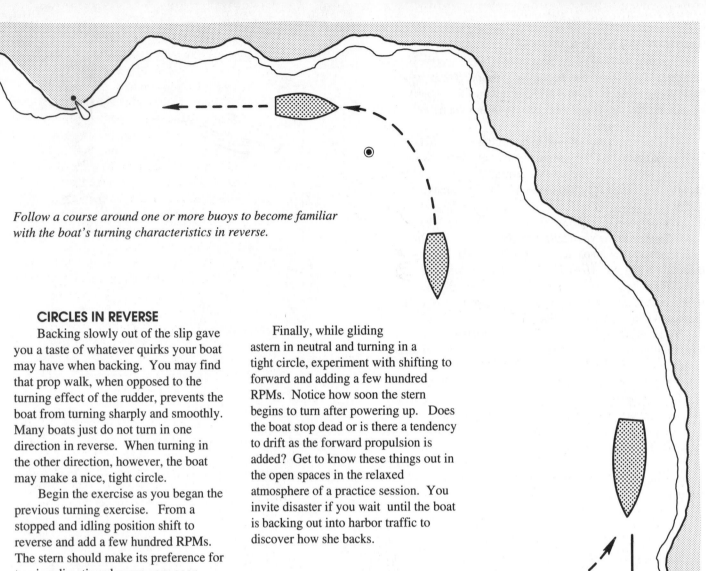

Follow a course around one or more buoys to become familiar with the boat's turning characteristics in reverse.

CIRCLES IN REVERSE

Backing slowly out of the slip gave you a taste of whatever quirks your boat may have when backing. You may find that prop walk, when opposed to the turning effect of the rudder, prevents the boat from turning sharply and smoothly. Many boats just do not turn in one direction in reverse. When turning in the other direction, however, the boat may make a nice, tight circle.

Begin the exercise as you began the previous turning exercise. From a stopped and idling position shift to reverse and add a few hundred RPMs. The stern should make its preference for turning directions known very soon. Once you determine which direction the stern kicks, turn the rudder in the opposite direction. The rudder turns more easily than in forward because water pushes the rudder to the side as the boat moves backward through the water. In severe cases force from water on rudder can slam the steering quadrant against it's stops, straining or breaking the system. It will stay hard over as long as the boat moves in reverse. In fact, turning it back will get more difficult as the boat moves faster and a greater volume of water pins the rudder in its position.

Repeat the procedure turning in the opposite direction. Note whether the turning circle is significantly smaller in one direction or the other. Also, when the boat is turning steadily in reverse, idle the engine down and shift into neutral. Notice the effect of turning without the force of the propeller. Try this while turning in both directions.

Finally, while gliding astern in neutral and turning in a tight circle, experiment with shifting to forward and adding a few hundred RPMs. Notice how soon the stern begins to turn after powering up. Does the boat stop dead or is there a tendency to drift as the forward propulsion is added? Get to know these things out in the open spaces in the relaxed atmosphere of a practice session. You invite disaster if you wait until the boat is backing out into harbor traffic to discover how she backs.

A three point turn in a confined area can pose a considerable challenge. Try the same maneuver from the opposite direction and you may discover quite different results.

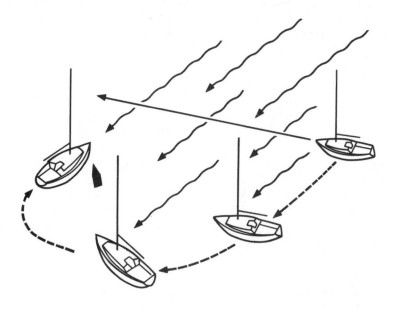

A strong current can force a helmsman to negotiate a turn altogether differently than he might in still water.

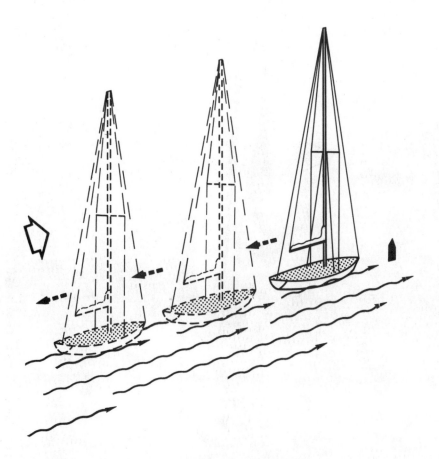

This boat must use reverse at high RPMs to oppose the forces of wind and current and stop near a marker.

WIND AND CURRENT

Backing out of the slip in Section I revealed cautions about navigating in the presence of these forces. Generally speaking, if the combined forces of the wind and current are opposed to your boat's direction, you would negotiate wider turns, perhaps turning later to allow for the added drift. When the combined force moves in the same direction, as you turn the boat more sharply, earlier, allowing the force to move you toward your destination.

While wind and current make motoring trickier, they can also help turn the boat once you understand how to use their effects. Practice will obviously require wind and/or current. You may have discovered that turning in reverse pits the propeller and rudder forces against one another. At times the wind and/or current may be necessary to allow the boat to turn within the available distance.

The following exercise requires a 10 knot or greater combination of wind and current. Begin making stern way into wind/current. Turn the wheel to the direction with the most sea room. Feel the effect of the wind on the hull as you bring it perpendicular to the wind. Wind across the bow will bring it downwind. This causes most boats to tend to back into the wind. If you discovered a direction the boat found difficult to turn in reverse, you may be able to use wind and current to overcome its resistance to turning in that direction.

Repeat all the exercises above in more wind and current so that you can begin to predict the effects of these conditions on your overall piloting.

Another valuable exercise uses reverse to turn the boat in a tighter radius while moving forward. In Section I you discovered prop walk and the boat's preference for turning to one side or the other in reverse. A right handed prop backs to port so your tightest turn in forward is to starboard. Begin turning in neutral. Shift occasionally into reverse and the stern will kick to port as a result. The boat turns more sharply to starboard as long as you use reverse sparingly and not long enough to stop the boat.

TOWING THE DINGHY

Dragging a dinghy behind a sailboat can be aggravating until the time comes to leave the anchored vessel and go snorkeling or visit the shore. So, like taxes and dentist appointments, we put up with the dinghy because we know it gives us great benefits despite the nuisance.

An inflatable dinghy should be deflated and stowed for anything but a short hop from one anchorage to another. Hard dinghies are often hoisted on deck and lashed down, a great opportunity to use your trucker's hitch. When either type dinghy must be towed, begin by inspecting the painter (towing line) and its attachment to the dinghy. Look for chafing along the line and especially at the point where it ties onto a "D" ring or pad eye on the dinghy. A safety line can be run to another hull attachment on the dinghy, led to a different cleat on the sailboat and left fairly slack. Lash or tape it to the painter to keep it out of the way. If the hull attachment or the painter fails, the dinghy remains attached to the boat.

People often spend hours dreamily looking ahead and to either side, but never backward. If the dinghy gets loose it can be miles back, well below the horizon, before anyone knows it is gone.

Take everything out of the dinghy which is not firmly attached. This includes oars, PFDs and snorkel gear. Bring the outboard and gas tank aboard the sailboat for anything but a short, calm coastal passage.

Motoring while towing the dinghy should not present any terribly sticky problems. Begin with one to two dinghy lengths of painter between the two boats. Increase boat speed gradually. When you reach cruising speed ease out more line. The dinghy puts quite a load on the painter so do not cast it off the cleat. Untie your cleat hitch but leave a full wrap around the cleat. Ease the line out using the cleat for friction. Watch the dinghy. When it gets about four dinghy lengths back, concentrate on positioning it so its bow rides higher than its stern. Then secure the line. The longer line will act as a shock absorber and the dinghy will ride smoother as it gets

further from the disturbance created by the sailboat moving through the water.

Sailing with a dinghy works the same way. Raise the sails with the dinghy in close. When the boat comes up to speed, ease the dinghy out until it rides comfortably behind the boat.

Having a dinghy astern adds a challenge when the time comes to maneuver in tight quarters. Anyone who has ever towed a car with another car has experienced the challenge of speeding up and slowing down two vehicles in unison. We have an advantage in that we can shorten the painter until the two boats are lashed tightly together. An inflatable will rest comfortably against your hull as long as none of its hardware makes contact. A hard dinghy needs plenty of fenders.

Pulling the dinghy right up on the center of the transom will minimize its effect on the sailboat's maneuverability. Attaching it on either side will cause a drag on that side of the boat. A small rudder adjustment compensates for the dinghy's drag when going forward. Reverse is another story. Drag has a

much greater effect. If the dinghy is only secured by its bow, it will flop to one side or the other when the boat goes astern. If you noticed a resistance to turning in one direction, tie the dinghy on that side of the boat. The added drag will help spin the stern in that direction while moving in reverse. Always assure that the dinghy is pulled up close to the stern before putting the propeller in reverse. If there is slack in the painter it will float under the boat and foul in the propeller, leaving you unable to maneuver.

SUMMARY

Many people who might benefit tremendously from the experience of sailing never step aboard a boat. They feel that the mass of rigging, cables, wires, tubes through-hulls and assorted other nautical paraphernalia far exceeds their ability to learn and command. Anyone who has progressed this far in *Cruising Fundamentals* knows differently. Everything connected with cruising a sailboat has a logical purpose and a manageable explanation. Your progress can be measured by a decreasing level of intimidation and an increased feeling of comfort. You have the ability to make the boat truly become an extension of yourself.

THE VOYAGE

"With sloping masts and dipping prow,
As who pursued with yell and blow
Still treads the shadow of his foe,
And forward bends his head,
The ship drove fast, loud roared the blast,
And southward aye we fled."

The Rime of the Ancient Mariner
— Samuel Taylor Coleridge

The portion of cruising time spent preparing, repairing or lying at anchor may exceed actual sailing time. It follows that learning sailboat cruising requires devoting time and attention to many things other than sailing. With luck, your fondness for cruising will extend to all the associated tasks necessary for successful cruising. Regardless, most evangelized sailors live for the rich simplicity of slicing through sapphire blue water before a fresh, warm breeze. Those treasured moments make the work and preparation worthwhile.

Section III provides your first opportunity to feel the symphonic harmony played out among the wind, boat and sails. Sailing Knowledge presents a variety of subjects which are likely to come into play while cruising under sail. Sailing Skills deals with sailing exercises on a larger boat. The knowledge and experience from the two previous sections will build confidence. Mastery of the boat's equipment and systems will free your attention to focus on the lessons at hand.

GALLEY PROCEDURES

Your galley tour in Section II introduced some of its components. Proper galley management will prevent injury, fire and spoilage, thereby, ensuring a safe and pleasant journey.

PROVISIONING

Buying staples for a cruise differs considerably from a trip to the market for your weekly groceries. Unlike your home, the boat may become subject to vigorous movement. Select unbreakable containers whenever possible. Avoid glass jars and bottles for things like mayonnaise or cooking oil. You may have to forego your favorite name brands, but that discomfort is slight compared to cleaning 20 ounces of ketchup and glass shards from behind the galley stove.

Delicate fruits and vegetables should be packed in small Tupperware-like containers. Shifting provisions, either in the ice box or a locker, will

crush any fragile items. Camping and boating stores sell hard plastic cases for egg storage. Also, eggs will last a surprisingly long time without refrigeration. Fresh citrus fruits and root vegetables, such as onions and potatoes, keep best if stowed in mesh bags that allow plenty of ventilation.

Packaging should be selected to minimize its volume of waste. Trash takes up valuable space that could otherwise be used for pleasurable purposes. While some space may be set aside specifically for trash storage, when the garbage expands beyond that area it steals space from something else. Containers that can be crushed and compacted help reduce trash.

Disposal of plastic at sea is illegal everywhere you can cruise a sailboat. Conscientious sailors keep all their trash until they can leave it in the proper shore-side receptacle.

REFRIGERATION

Your inspection of the galley and electrical panels has revealed the boat's options for refrigeration. A good stock of ice will bring the ice box temperature down and keep it down; but ice may melt quickly in warm weather. Once away from the dock, any electrical or mechanical refrigeration system will require running the engine. We accept the engine's noise and vibration while coming in and out of harbors or in times of inadequate breeze, but sailing with the engine banging defeats the purpose of sailing in the first place. Adapt your supply of perishables to conform to your boat's refrigeration capabilities, the availability of ice and the crew's willingness to listen to the engine.

Most charter companies offer a choice of two provision packages. Split provisions include breakfast, lunch and snacks for the specified crew size and cruise duration. Full provisions also include dinner. Selecting split provisions allows a charterer to enjoy exploring new and exotic places, eating ashore and shopping for local delicacies. A variety of snacks

and drinks comes with each plan. Beer, wine and spirits are usually the responsibility of the charter clients.

Charter companies usually provide a menu for the provisions on the boat. They cleverly plan to use the perishable items, such as milk or some fruits, in the first few days and leave the food with most endurance for later. Follow this same rule or, if possible, acquire a sample provision/menu list from a charter company. Modify it to suit the needs of your crew and save a lot of valuable time by not re-inventing a smoothly turning wheel.

You will discover that with the exception of some larger boats, galley ice boxes load from the top through a relatively small opening. Shelves may create some helpful options for stowing goods; but, invariably, many things are stacked on top of one another. Any good grocery clerk knows that the hard, heavy things like cans go on the bottom of the bag and more delicate products like bread go on the top. Stowing ice boxes the same way prevents damage to fragile items. Unfortunately, some heavy things such as cans of soda and other drinks are more frequently pulled from the box. Stacking them on the bottom, where they logically belong, means moving everything above every time someone reaches for a drink.

A vertical partition, as simple as a small piece of plywood, can create a wall between items which should be kept segregated. Alternately, bring a picnic cooler, stock it with drinks and ice and stow it in an accessible place. Also, bring plenty of snack items like nuts or dried fruit which can be stowed in a galley locker for easy access. The sometimes tight placement of food in the ice box will not be disrupted nor will the cold escape from frequent opening and closing.

Even the most enthusiastic cooks find the galley confining and usually prefer other pursuits while on passage. Preparing meals in advance preserves more time for leisure. It also reduces the frustration of cooking in an inadequately stocked, cramped galley. Casseroles such as lasagna, Stroganoff or stew can be cooked and frozen in a suitable container at home. When the charter trip begins with an airplane ride, pack an inexpensive Styrofoam ice chest and carry it on the plane. Even with minimal refrigeration these meals will defrost gradually in the ice box and keep for days after they thaw. They need only be heated at meal time.

Camping and marine stores sell sealed meals that adventurers find popular. One variety requires no reconstituting. Plastic wrappers containing the food are placed in boiling water for a short time and then served. Dehydrated provisions are also very practical on boats because they are light and take up very little space. Neither type of food requires refrigeration. Another modern product to include in galley planning is UHT (Ultra High Temperature) milk, which compares well to fresh milk but requires no refrigeration until after the box has been opened.

Hinged doors cut into counter tops provide access to cold storage without giving up counter space.

THE GALLEY STOVE

The three most common fuel sources for cooking on board are alcohol, liquified petroleum gas (LPG or propane) and compressed natural gas (CNG). Each has clear advantages and disadvantages. Fire on a boat can spread incredibly fast and fire is one of your most dreaded enemies. Always take great care to understand your cooking source and operate it with caution. Instruct all crew members on stove operation and safety. Keep a fire extinguisher in the galley at all times and be sure it is mounted where it can be reached easily if there is a fire on the stove.

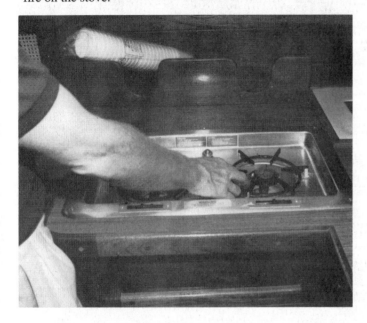

STOVE IDENTIFICATION

There are two types of alcohol stoves; those with a pressurized alcohol supply and those whose alcohol is not delivered to the burner under pressure. Non-pressurized systems are fairly simple and usually have directions printed on the unit. Both types are fueled by liquid alcohol which turns to vapor when heated.

Stoves that use pressurized alcohol are most common. Their burners have many tiny holes around a dome-shaped mantle in its center. A metal collar or cup sits below the mantle. It catches alcohol escaping in liquid form and is used to pre-heat the burner unit. (see steps 5 and 6 at right).

The alcohol stove pictured here has its fuel fill and pressure pump on the stove itself. Larger stoves, some equipped with ovens, get fuel from a reservoir tank. A bicycle tire pump supplies pressure to the tank. Follow the fuel line to the tank. A valve similar to one found on a bicycle tire will help identify alcohol systems.

Both types of gas stove draw fuel from highly pressurized tanks. You may need to rely on tank and stove labeling for fuel identification. Tanks are generally kept in a vented cockpit locker. Propane is heavier than air and will collect in the bottom of a locker or the bilge. CNG is lighter than air and could collect high in the cabin or the top of a locker. Propane tank lockers should be vented overboard at the bottom and CNG tanks should have a vent at the top or a loosely fitting lid.

ALCOHOL STOVE OPERATION

Alcohol can be stored as a liquid at room temperature without pressurization. Its vapor dissipates in air rather than collecting in pockets. The flame is difficult to see and not as hot as gas and it requires some care while lighting. Following these simple steps can eliminate most problems.

1. **Release pressure from the system.** The two-burner stove has a small cap on top for adding fuel. **Slowly** unscrew the cap and listen for escaping pressure. The valve on a reservoir tank works just like the valve stem on a car or bicycle tire. Depress the tiny pin in the middle of the valve with a tool. A screw driver or a finger nail will do nicely. Keep the pin depressed until pressure no longer escapes. This type of tank is often fitted with a pressure gauge. It takes the guess work out of pressurizing and releasing pressure.

2. **Check alcohol level.** Remove the filler cap and use something like a pencil to dip into the alcohol fill pipe to determine the fuel level. Marine stores sell stove fuel specifically formulated for use with the stove. Unlike some other available forms of alcohol, stove fuel has an additive which gives it color when burned. Add alcohol if necessary. Leave at least 1/4 of the available tank volume for air space.

3. **Close all valves.** Make sure all burner and oven valves have been turned clockwise until they stop.

4. **Replace the cap and pressurize the system.** Pump the plunger on a small stove 15 to 20 times or attach the bicycle pump to the valve on a larger stove and bring the pressure gauge up to 15 to 20 pounds of pressure.

5. **Open the tank valve.** Stoves with reservoir tanks may have a petcock on the fitting which leads out of the tank. Turn it 90° counterclockwise to open.

6. **Prime the pre-heat cup.** Quickly open and close the knob on the burner you wish to light until a small amount of alcohol escapes into the cup beneath the burner. Release only enough alcohol to cover the bottom of the cup, not more than a couple of teaspoonfuls.

7. **Pre-heat the burner.** The alcohol stove burner works by heating the liquid alcohol inside the mantle and transforming it to a vapor before it reaches the flame. Ignite the alcohol in the cup to initially heat the mantle. A few minutes of healthy flame should do the trick.

8. **Turn on the burner.** After the flame in the cup has died down, turn the burner up and a clean, pressurized, gas-like flame will appear. It can be adjusted up or down according to your needs.

(continued)

You will recognize the proper flame by the sound it makes, similar to a steadily hissing torch or a jet engine. If the tall, lazy flame re-appears when you turn the burner on, or if there is a sputtering sound accompanied by brief flare-ups, turn it off and allow the burner to pre-heat longer. When the flame subsides, try turning the burner on again. The oven heats with a burner identical to the ones on the cook top. Alcohol fires can usually be extinguished with large quantities of water. Keep a pan with water handy in case the stove flame gets out of control. Also, the tall, lazy flames created by burning raw alcohol in the cup can be controlled by placing a pan of water on the burner. This saves curtains and eye brows from scorching.

Turn the burner off by closing the control knob. If the burner is still hot from previous use, it can be relighted without pre-heating. Open the valve and put a match to the burner. If liquid alcohol appears, start over with the pre-heating sequence. When finished using the stove, turn all burners off. Let them cool for a few minutes, then release any remaining pressure from the fuel tank.

Place a pan of water on an alcohol stove flare-up to help control the flame until excess fuel has been consumed.

A gauge on the cylinder indicates fuel level in pounds per square inch. It will give a reading on a charged cylinder when the valve attached to the cylinder has been opened.

GAS STOVE OPERATION

Gas stoves and ovens are more popular than alcohol because temperature and flames are more controllable and they require no pre-heating. They do require extra caution because of their volatility and pressurized gas.

Propane systems usually have a solenoid switch for emergency shut-off. It stops the flow of propane immediately when switched to the off position. Your previous inspection of the galley discussed its location.

Follow these instructions for safe operation of either propane or CNG stoves.

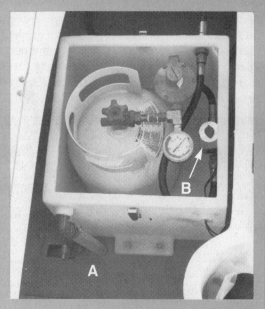

Stove fuel (CNG and LPG) tanks are often stowed in containment lockers. With a lid in place, any escaping gas will be diverted overboard through the vent tube (A). The electric solenoid valve (B) is controlled by a switch in the cabin.

1. **Ventilate the cabin and run the bilge blower.** Never light the stove immediately after boarding a boat whose hatches have been tightly closed. Allow at least 5 minutes for ventilation.

2. **Turn all burners off.** All knobs on the stove should be turned clockwise until they stop.

3. **Open the tank valve.** A screw-down type handle controls the flow of gas from the tank. Turn it 1/4 turn counter clockwise and you will hear a short burst of gas pressure. The needle on the gauge will also react to the pressure release if the tank was turned off and the system de-pressurized.

4. **Turn on the solenoid switch.** A light on the switch panel will indicate when the switch is on. This allows gas to flow from the tank to the stove.

5. **Ignite the burner.** Some stoves have self-igniting burners. Turn the knob beyond the "High" setting and it will make a clicking sound as sparks are generated to ignite the burner without a flame. Otherwise, use a match or lighter.

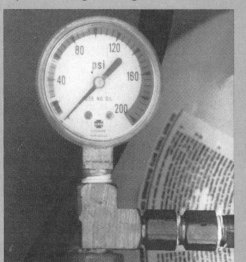

While cooking, be especially careful not to turn the burner down so low the flame goes out. This could let unburned gas escape until a source of ignition sets it off with explosive results.

When finished cooking with a gas stove, turn off all but one burner. Turn off the solenoid switch and watch the last burner go out as the residual gas burns. Turn off the burner and the supply at the tank.

COOKING SAFETY

The errant flame from any stove can best be controlled by removing the fuel source. The burner knobs, the solenoid and the tank valve will stop the gas flow but if something else has caught fire, act quickly to prevent the situation from getting out of hand. Water may not be the best way to fight a fire. Burning oil in a pan, for example, might just splash out and spread to other parts of the boat. In that case, extinguish the fire by removing the source of oxygen. Cover the pan with a tight lid.

A fire extinguisher may be the best way to get fires out fast; but remember that the mess created by a dry chemical fire extinguisher takes a great deal of effort to clean up (See Fire Fighting, Section V)

Cooking presents one of the greatest dangers in the galley because it combines flames with the movement of the boat and places the cook in a confined area surrounded by potential projectiles. Strapping oneself into the galley can prevent a thrashing in turbulent waters. Utensils and containers should always be returned to a secure locker when not in use.

Oversized pots and pans are recommended for heating food and water. Allow extra room at the top and use covers whenever possible. Bibbed foul weather pants will protect the most vulnerable parts of your body in the event something hot flies in your direction. Never leave a lighted galley stove unattended. Keep a constant watch to guard against flare-ups, spills, blown-out burner flames and other mishaps that can have damaging consequences.

Heavy foul weather gear pants protect the body's most vulnerable parts from scalding while cooking.

Soapy water applied to pressurized lines will bubble in the presence of a leak.

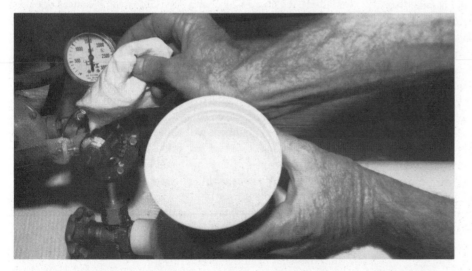

GALLEY SINK

Sometimes crew members who cook in kitchens with garbage disposals have difficulty adjusting to the galley. Its drain is vulnerable to more than just silverware. Debris will clog it quickly and grease will cool and harden into an effective plug. Dishes, pots and pans should be scraped free of solids which go into the trash. Nothing more solid than soapy dishwater should go into the galley sink.

Take great care to see that the strainer/plug is in place while using the sink. If the sink fails to drain, a careful massage with a finger tip in the drain opening might dislodge obstructions; but watch out for sharp objects like broken glass. Opening and closing the through-hull may release debris on that end. A wire snake, very carefully worked into the drain, could help clear up a problem. Don't put liquid or solid drain openers into the galley sink drain. Never pour anything stronger than bleach into the drain.

SEA SICKNESS

There are a few basic rules about the disquieting condition the French refer to as "mal de mer" and we simply call sea sickness.

Rule number 1 — anyone could fall victim to the disease under the right (or wrong) circumstances.

Rule number 2 — during a severe bout of this illness very little else matters, not finances, not romance, not even life itself.

Rule number 3 — it is possible for those afflicted with recurring sea sickness to fight it medically and even build a tolerance.

Sea sickness, in layman's terms, is confusion within the brain, caused by contradictory signals between the inner ear and the eyes. The inner ear which controls our sense of physical balance recognizes motion which the eyes may not. The results of this confusion are fatigue, dizziness and nausea.

The following factors might cause or aggravate sea sickness:

- Fatigue
- Minor illness such as a head cold or flu
- Consumption of heavy, greasy food
- Acidic beverages like citrus
- Alcohol consumption
- Nervousness and worry about getting sick
- Unpleasant aromas (diesel fuel, gasoline)
- Some prescription drugs
- Excess time below deck

Start a voyage in good health whenever possible. Rest well and stick to a light, relatively bland diet for several days before departure. Some sailors are blessed and never experience any form of sea sickness. Never take medication, prescription or not, without having some history of discomfort.

Most motion sickness drugs have side effects including drowsiness, blurred vision and dryness of the mouth. Try the medication and dosage you plan to take on land during the weeks prior to the voyage to check for adverse effects. Remember on the day of departure that most of these medications are intended to prevent rather than cure sea sickness. They must be in your system prior to departure to have their intended effect.

A number of motion sickness remedies are available without prescription. Ask a pharmacist which over-the-counter medication best suits your needs and the needs of the crew. Transderm-Scop®, a prescription medication, has become popular among sailors. It comes in the form of a patch which attaches behind the ear. It is effective for about three days, by which time most people have acquired their "sea legs" (and stomach). Always consult a physician before administering this or any other prescription drug.

Anyone experiencing signs of sea sickness should be brought into the open air immediately. Encourage the person to focus on land or the horizon. A stable, visual reference often helps orient a deteriorating individual. Some of those afflicted will experience great fatigue and sleep until the boat makes

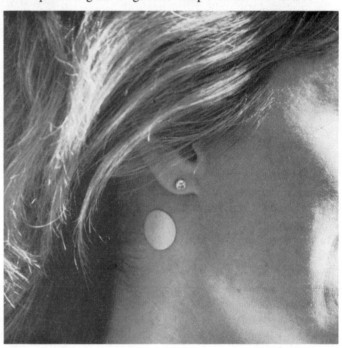

landfall. Open air is probably advisable even if nausea does not occur.

A glass of water, biscuits, crackers or bread may settle a churning stomach, but don't force the issue because a person may be rejecting food or drink for very good reasons. Encourage anyone who has thrown up to drink small amounts of water or non-cola soda to fight dehydration.

In all but extreme cases a combination of precautions, medication and treatment will help win the battle against the debilitating discomfort of sea sickness. The body can acclimate to the marine environment with caution and practice.

Eventually, even a dull, nagging reminder of your stomach's displeasure will give way to another, more immediate craving; hunger. At that point the battle between your ears and your digestive system has either gone in your favor or, at least, reached a stand-off. You should expect improvement from that point forward.

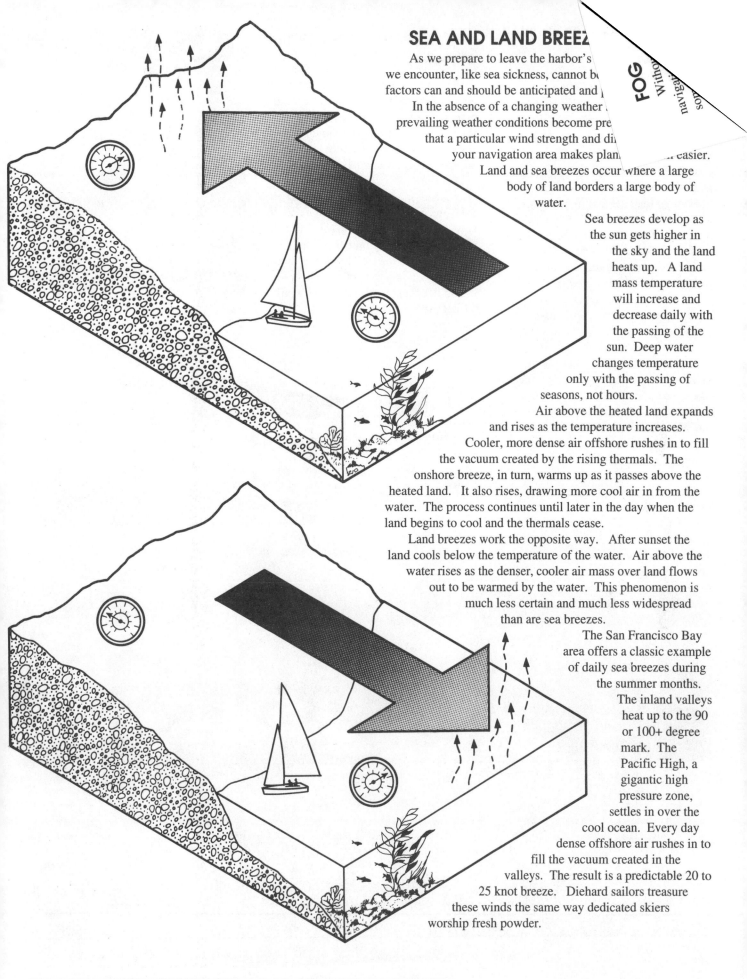

SEA AND LAND BREEZ

As we prepare to leave the harbor's
we encounter, like sea sickness, cannot b
factors can and should be anticipated and

In the absence of a changing weather
prevailing weather conditions become pre
that a particular wind strength and di
your navigation area makes plan   easier.

Land and sea breezes occur where a large
body of land borders a large body of
water.

Sea breezes develop as
the sun gets higher in
the sky and the land
heats up. A land
mass temperature
will increase and
decrease daily with
the passing of the
sun. Deep water
changes temperature
only with the passing of
seasons, not hours.

Air above the heated land expands
and rises as the temperature increases.
Cooler, more dense air offshore rushes in to fill
the vacuum created by the rising thermals. The
onshore breeze, in turn, warms up as it passes above the
heated land.   It also rises, drawing more cool air in from the
water. The process continues until later in the day when the
land begins to cool and the thermals cease.

Land breezes work the opposite way.   After sunset the
land cools below the temperature of the water. Air above the
water rises as the denser, cooler air mass over land flows
out to be warmed by the water. This phenomenon is
much less certain and much less widespread
than are sea breezes.

The San Francisco Bay
area offers a classic example
of daily sea breezes during
the summer months.

The inland valleys
heat up to the 90
or 100+ degree
mark. The
Pacific High, a
gigantic high
pressure zone,
settles in over the
cool ocean. Every day
dense offshore air rushes in to
fill the vacuum created in the
valleys. The result is a predictable 20 to
25 knot breeze. Diehard sailors treasure
these winds the same way dedicated skiers
worship fresh powder.

... the luxury of sight, ... on becomes dangerous and ... etimes terrifying. Channel entrances, buoys, rocks, boats and other obstructions are easily negotiated with clear vision. Darkness limits our vision but lighted navigation aids, lighted onshore landmarks and running lights help us find our way without much difficulty. Imagine finding your way into a harbor blindfolded! Fog creates a blindfold of sorts but it can be predicted once you understand its causes, and it can be conquered by the measures a prudent sailor takes to avoid problems.

All air, even in the desert, has water vapor suspended in it. Air at higher temperatures can hold a greater volume of water vapor than cooler air can. Air is said to be saturated when it can hold no more water vapor. Dew point refers to a temperature at which the air mass becomes saturated and invisible moisture condenses and becomes visible. Fog forms when innumerable water droplets condense and become visible yet float suspended in the air.

Radiation fog occurs over land at night. Heat escapes from the earth into the clear sky, cooling the ground. The ground cools the air directly above it when it is below its dew point and fog occurs. The fog is limited to the cooled air close to the ground; warmer air a bit higher stays above the dew point and is fog free. Radiation fog will not occur during periods of high winds because the wind mixes the air and prevents creation of a cool layer close to the ground. Radiation fog can spread over a body of water that is sufficiently cool to keep the air temperature below its dew point. It tends to burn off over land as the sun rises higher in the sky but cold water can delay the process. The conditions necessary for radiation fog usually occur at night and in late summer and fall.

Advection fog can develop in any season and at any time of the day or night. It occurs when warm, moist air moves over a surface cool enough to drop its temperature below the dew point. Unlike radiation fog, it can be accompanied by winds and persist for prolonged periods.

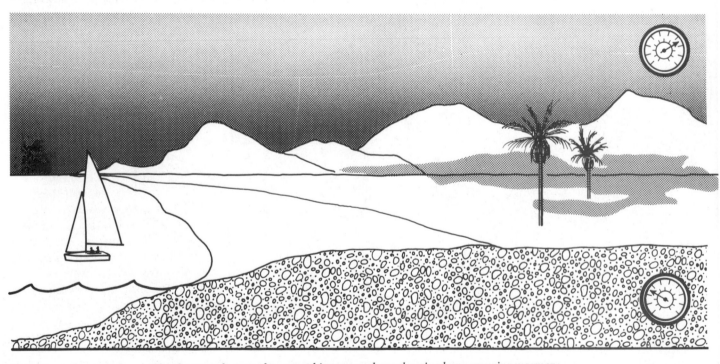

Warmer, moist air from above the water turns to fog as it blows over the cooler land.

Fog forms only near the ground in areas where the air above remains warmer.

NAVIGATING IN FOG

Although the technology exists to predict fog, consider it something that occurs when you least expect it. Sometimes in the matter of an instant, fog will set in and your vision will become completely obscured. A series of actions, calmly executed, will maximize your safety and ensure that the situation remains only an inconvenience.

1. **Reduce speed.** Your boat's speed should match the visibility. If your bow lookout cannot see more than one boat length ahead, speed should be at a minimum. Sailing interferes less than motoring with the crew's ability to hear other vessels, navigation aids, waves on shore or other obstructions. Either shorten sail or ease the throttle back. Do not just sit and wait. A boat cannot maneuver to avoid collision unless it has some way on (bare steerage way at least).

2. **Update navigation.** Fix your position as accurately as possible; then keep a very close watch on your chartwork, especially when the boat approaches land or a recognizable charted object.

3. **Post a lookout on the bow.**

4. **Turn on navigation lights**. The glow of running lights might attract more attention than the non-illuminated hull, sails and spars. The rules require navigation lights during any time of reduced visibility.

5. **Make sound signals.** The federal Navigation Rules require vessels to use their sound making device (probably a horn) to alert other vessels of their presence. The type of signal indicates the type of boat and its situation. A "short blast" lasts about one second and a "prolonged blast" lasts 4 to 6 seconds. If you are motoring, consider your boat "a power driven vessel making way through the water" and

you "shall sound at intervals of not more than 2 minutes one prolonged blast."

"A power driven vessel underway but stopped...shall sound at intervals of not more than 2 minutes two prolonged blasts in succession with an interval of about 2 seconds between them."

A sailing vessel shall "sound at intervals of not more than 2 minutes three blasts in succession, namely one prolonged followed by two short blasts."

Knowing the correct signals also gives you the advantage of recognizing them when you hear other vessels signaling. Vessels 40 feet and larger must carry a copy of the Navigation Rules, published by the U. S. Coast Guard. All boaters are advised to obtain a copy of the rules and have them handy while underway.

6. **Hoist a radar reflector.** A sailboat, like a stealth bomber, presents few surfaces that reflect a radar signal to a vessel using its radar. You may be invisible and vulnerable to a collision, especially if the other vessel moves at high speed. A radar reflector, placed high in the rigging, greatly increases the size of your boat's image on a ship's radar screen.

7. **Place the crew in PFDs.** This may not be the most prudent public relations move but it is prudent seamanship.

Anchoring may be an option in acceptable conditions. Anchor well out of the way of any normal traffic lanes. Never anchor in a channel. Anchoring out might be preferable to navigating into a busy commercial harbor, but only when the anchorage itself presents no danger.

The Navigation Rules state that "A vessel at anchor shall at intervals of not more than one minute ring the bell rapidly for about 5 seconds." Also, "A vessel of less than 12 meters (40 feet) in length shall not be obliged to give the above mentioned signals but, if she does not, shall make some other efficient sound signal at intervals of not more than 2 minutes."

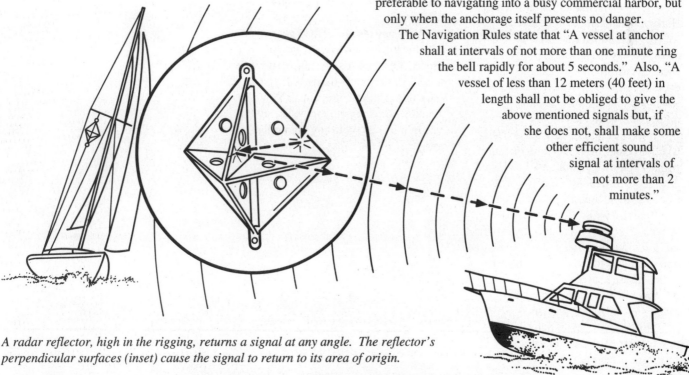

A radar reflector, high in the rigging, returns a signal at any angle. The reflector's perpendicular surfaces (inset) cause the signal to return to its area of origin.

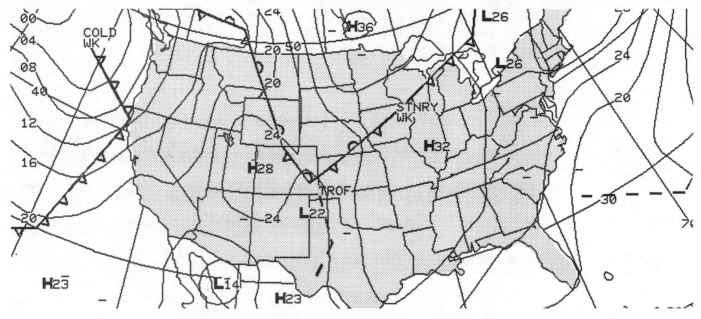

A synoptic weather chart indicates areas of low and high pressure as well as the movements of cold and warm fronts.

WEATHER PREDICTION

Although most weather predictions come from the same U. S. government source, prudent sailors check a variety of sources before a voyage of any length. If your trip takes you away from home port for over a day or two you may want to consult sources other than NOAA radio on the VHF. They could provide valuable additional information. Hurricanes and some other severe weather conditions can often be predicted days in advance. Early warning can provide invaluable help in avoiding problems. The following are some possible alternate weather information sources.

Recorded telephone weather. Dial local directory assistance or look in the phone book for the number of 24 hour a day recorded weather. It may not be available in all areas.

Television and radio broadcasts. Weather forecasts on television and radio stations are often more specific to particular areas than NOAA weather radio. These sources of weather information may also offer a longer range view of future weather.

Newspapers. Most daily newspapers list local and national forecasts. The chart above is an example of a typical chart found in many newspapers. A detailed forecast should also accompany the chart.

Airports. Most airports, even those servicing smaller aircraft, can provide detailed local weather information. Sometimes the Federal Aviation Administration office will provide the information. Otherwise it may take a few calls to connect with the right office.

You may also be able to get valuable local knowledge from the airport. Officials may be able to provide details on weather patterns and typical wind strengths and directions. You should make every attempt to secure this type of information in any unfamiliar area.

ASSISTANCE TO OTHERS

The tradition of courtesy and charity extends far beyond the race course. Early explorers and warriors who set off by ship to conquer the world recognized their vulnerability in an environment that showed them nothing much kinder than ambivalence. You bear a legal responsibility for rendering assistance to a fellow boater in distress. Listed below are the recognized distress signals.

Boaters displaying any of these signals are most likely in need of some kind of help. Although you cannot abandon fellow boaters in need, prudence should prevail when assessing your ability to render assistance. Though rare, unscrupulous individuals have feigned distress to take advantage of rescuers. Approach a disabled vessel with caution and use good judgment when appraising the situation. In an extreme case you may not safely be able to do more than radio for law enforcement or a private towing company and stand by until help arrives.

A distressed vessel may need fuel or other supplies such as medical equipment. You may choose to donate your spare fuel but do so only if this will leave you adequate fuel to reach port. A transfusion shouldn't kill the donor to save the recipient. Syphoning or otherwise removing fuel from your tanks is messy and dangerous; avoid it. Commercial towing companies will bring fuel to a distressed boat and this may provide the safest, most practical solution. They can be hailed on VHF channel 16. (Specific calling instructions follow in the Sailing Skills of this section) Bandages or other medical supplies may help ease an injured person's pain and should be given up readily. Water, food, clothing or other provisions should be shared according to the needs of the other vessel and the capabilities of your vessel to do without. Never risk the well being of your crew or boat unnecessarily.

TOWING

Offering a tow may be the best way to help a disabled vessel. The following tips can make towing easier and safer.

Select a sturdy line. The stresses placed on the towing hawser exceed other loads that normal sailing places on a line. The anchor rode may be your best choice.

Check knots and chafe points. Knots that join two lines or fasten a line to a cleat should be tied carefully and double checked. Lead lines through bow chocks or the anchor roller to reduce chafing.

Keep crew clear of the tow line. When a line parts under great strain it snaps like a giant rubber band. Stay well clear of the hawser.

Gather speed slowly. Allow the towed boat to gain speed by accelerating gradually. Be prepared to reduce speed quickly if the towed boat experiences any difficulty.

Keep boats in step. Adjust the towing hawser so both boats are at the same position on the waves or swells.

If your boat needs towing, make sure to establish what, if any, compensation the towing boat's skipper expects. Maritime law governs your actions at sea and some strange rules have surfaced in the area of towing and salvage. Your savior's intentions should be crystal clear before you accept his kindness.

Emergency distress signals

RESPONSIBILITIES

The skipper, like any boss, assumes responsibility for the boat's entire operation. Legally, the master of the vessel must answer to authorities if complications arise during a voyage. Ignorance of this fact or any other applicable law is never considered an adequate defense.

The skipper's responsibilities fall into two broad categories: safety of the crew and safety of the vessel. The highest priority goes to safety of the crew. Most injuries aboard ship can and should be avoided. The skipper's greater experience and more developed judgment should act as a guiding force in maintaining a safe shipboard environment. Crew are not always aware of potential hazards. The skipper must assume the responsibility of preventing accidents. The skipper must train the crew, delegate appropriate responsibility and monitor and evaluate performance.

Safety of the ship is the skipper's other area of responsibility. Daredevils and risk takers will eventually meet their match if they sail long enough. The sea simply doesn't know and doesn't care about the brave or foolhardy sailor. All the skippers' decisions must be made with this thought in mind.

The crew bears a less critical, but no less important, set of responsibilities. In short, crew must obey the captain. Specifically, the crew must accept and carry out to the best of their ability, the responsibilities the captain delegates to them. For example, captain and crew share responsibility for the ship in a case where the helm and lookout positions have been assigned to crew members. The captain may not even be on deck, but by assigning individuals who are competent under the existing circumstances, he has carried out his duty. The crew in turn must follow the captain's orders which always require, explicitly or implicitly, safe operation of the vessel. When the demands of a situation exceed the crew's experience, the crew has a duty to inform the skipper of that fact. The responsibility then reverts back to the skipper.

FLOAT PLAN

Always leave a float plan with a friend or relative before leaving on any voyage. Include a complete description of the vessel including length, color, trim, type of vessel and registration numbers. List the number of people on board, their names, addresses and telephone numbers. A complete itinerary should accompany the float plan. Also include the time and date to contact authorities if the vessel has not returned and the telephone number of the appropriate authorities. The form on the next page should be photocopied for further use.

FLOAT PLAN

Complete this page, before going boating and leave it with a reliable person who you can be depended upon to notify the Coast Guard or other rescue organization, should you not return as scheduled. Do not file this plan with the Coast Guard.

1. Name of person reporting and telephone number.

_____

2. Description of boat. Type _____

Color _____ Trim _____

Registration Number _____

Length _____ Name_____

Make _____

Other Information _____

3. Number of Persons Aboard _____

Name _____ Age _____

Address_____

Telephone Number _____

Name _____ Age _____

Address_____

Telephone Number _____

Name _____ Age _____

Address_____

Telephone Number _____

4. Do any of the persons aboard have a medical problem? If so, What? _____

5. Engine Type_____

H.P. _____ # of Engines _____ Fuel Capacity _____

6. Survival equipment: (Check as Appropriate and Indicate Number)

❑ PFDs _____   ❑ Flares _____   ❑ Mirror _____

❑ Smoke Signals _____   ❑ Flashlight _____

❑ Food _____

_____

❑ Paddles _____   ❑ Water _____   ❑ Anchors _____

❑ Dinghy _____   ❑ EPIRB _____   ❑ Other _____

7. Radio Yes/No Type _____

Frequencies _____

8. Trip Expectations: Leaving at _____

From _____

_____

Going To _____

_____

Date_____

Going To _____

_____

Date_____

Going To _____

_____

Date_____

Going To _____

_____

Date_____

Expect to Return By (time) _____

and in no Event Later Than_____

9. Any Other Pertinent Information_____

_____

10. Automobile License Type_____

Trailer License_____

Color and Make of Auto _____

Where Parked _____

11. If Not Returned by (date & time) _____

_____

Call the Coast Guard, or _____

(local authority) _____

12. Telephone Numbers_____

_____

FLAG ETIQUETTE

Look at any marina and you will notice that the concentration of flags exceeds almost any place on earth except possibly the United Nations. Flags aboard boats seem randomly arranged at first glance but, like most things in the world of boats, an order exists. The type and placement of flags makes a difference.

NATIONAL FLAG

The flag of the boat's country of registry should be flown off the stern, either from the backstay or on a flagstaff (usually a wooden pole, held in place by a metal bracket). Remember, when chartering from companies based outside the U. S. the boat's home country flag should remain at the stern. While the "yacht ensign" (fouled anchor and circle of stars in the blue field of the U. S. flag) can legally be flown by documented yachts in U. S. waters, only the familiar "stars and stripes" should be flown by U. S. vessels in international and foreign waters.

HOST COUNTRY FLAG

When traveling in the waters of another country the flag of the host country should be hoisted to the starboard spreader. In the case of a ketch, yawl or schooner, the host country flag flies from the starboard spreader of the forwardmost mast.

Mexican flag hoisted by a U. S. vessel while visiting Mexico.

COURTESY TO RACERS

It should be clearly understood that, despite their often vigorous insistence otherwise, racing sailors have no more preferential status than that granted other vessels under the Navigation Rules. You would be within your rights to reply to the oft heard threat, "We're racing!" by saying "We're cruising" and leave it at that.

Try to avoid such temptations. In modern times, sailors have a tradition of courtesy and charity to one another. In most cases there is at least one navigational alternative to sailing through a start or finish line or impeding a boat's progress on a race course. Try to exercise that option and stay clear of the race. Racers usually appreciate your efforts to avoid being one more obstacle to their elusive goal of victory at sea.

SECTION III
REVIEW QUESTIONS

1. _____ is lighter than air and could collect high in the cabin or the top of a locker.

2. Alcohol fires can usually be extinguished with large quantities of _____.

3. Propane systems usually have a _____ for emergency shut-off.

4. Opening and closing the _____ may release debris that prevents the galley sink from draining.

5. A sea sick person should focus visually on _____ or the _____.

6. _____ breezes develop as the sun gets higher in the sky and the land heats up.

7. _____ fog occurs over land at night as heat escapes from the earth into the clear sky, cooling the ground.

8. A "short blast" lasts about _____ and a "prolonged blast" lasts _____.

9. When traveling in the waters of another country the flag of _____ should be hoisted to the starboard spreader.

10. The _____ is responsible for the safety of the crew and vessel.

Circle the correct true or false answers below

11. True or false? Disposal of plastic is legal beyond three miles from the U. S. mainland.

12. True or false? Alcohol can be stored as a liquid at room temperature without pressurization.

13. True or false? A sailing vessel sounds three signals in the fog.

14. True or false? Commercial towing companies can be reached on VHF channel 16.

15. True or false? Racing yachts have the right-of-way under the International Rules.

SAILING SKILLS

The larger, heavier boat, with or without additional sails, handles differently than a smaller boat. Turning, accelerating, slowing down and stopping all require some adjustment on your part. Lines that were trimmed by a casual tug now require winching. The following exercises will help small boat sailors adjust to the feel of sailing a bigger boat.

> *Always sail with the gear shift in neutral or reverse*

BEARING AWAY

With the sails raised (see Section I) put the boat on the wind and sail close hauled. Your experience with the helm thus far has been under power. Heaviness, created by water forced past the rudder from the propeller, disappears under sail. The leverage created by a large diameter wheel coupled with the absence of propeller wash makes most modern sailboats very delicate at the helm.

Practice holding the boat "in the slot" where the telltales all flow smoothly aft. Experiment with the amount of helm force necessary to stall the windward telltale.

Bear away to a close reach. When the masthead fly and helmsman agree that this point of sail has been achieved, trim

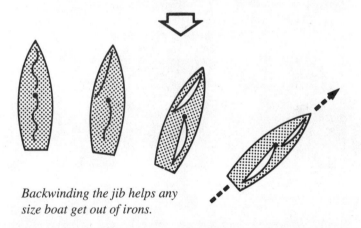

Backwinding the jib helps any size boat get out of irons.

the sails. Notice the amount of tension the existing wind strength places on the sheets. Paying out the tail with the right hand while holding the coils tight on the winch drum with the left adds control. The left hand can rotate the coils slowly, allowing only a few inches of line out at a time. It also keeps the sheet secure while removing coils from the winch. Wear sailing gloves whenever your on-deck duties call for handling lines.

Continue bearing away to a beam reach. The heeling angle decreases as apparent wind moves aft. The wind strength across the deck also diminishes. Sailing close hauled adds nearly all of the boat's speed to the wind velocity. The wind strength experienced on the boat increases by perhaps 4 to 6 knots in a fresh breeze. That apparent wind speed decreases as you bear away. The load on your sheets also eases, making sail handling easier.

Bear away to a broad reach and continue feeling out the boat. Determine whether the boom vang doubles as a preventer as it often does on smaller boats. Hydraulic vangs will not. Begin heading up and repeat the bearing away exercise in reverse. Notice the amount of effort required to trim sheets on each speed of a two speed winch. Helmsman and trimmer can coordinate their actions. The helmsman may luff up slightly to reduce strain on the sheets and make trimming easier.

COMING ABOUT

The familiar commands of "ready about" and "helm's a lee" do not change on a larger boat. The boat's reaction to tacking may differ quite a bit. Prepare for a tack by positioning a crew member at each jib sheet winch. The crew member assigned to the lazy sheet puts two or three wraps on the winch and reports "ready". The working sheet is flaked out and laying in the cockpit away from hands and feet. The working sheet crew will reply "ready" when the sheet has been uncleated or eased out of the self-tailer. Be very careful not to ease the tension on the working sheet. It is probably under an extreme load. It can easily pull the crew's hand into the winch or burn the skin. Premature easing of the sheet will also spill wind and power from the sail. Holding the coils against the drum with the left hand should keep the sheet from running out.

Timing becomes critical when tacking a large jib. Sheets on a small boat can be released at just about any time before coming head to weather. The greater force on the larger sail pulls the sheet violently away from the winch. The crew who releases the working sheet must pay attention and uncoil the sheet from the drum as the jib begins to luff and the load is momentarily eased. The sheet should come entirely off the winch as quickly as possible and the crew should watch the sheet run through the blocks and be prepared to release it if it becomes fouled.

The crew on the new working sheet will discover that its increased length calls for a lot more tailing. You intentionally wrapped only 2 or 3 coils on the drum to minimize the risk of an override. During a tack the loose coils of a slackened sheet can wander up and down the winch drum. One coil may slip underneath another and become trapped when the sheet tightens. Fewer wraps reduce the chance of getting an override or "bad wrap". When an override occurs try to free it by working the tail out from under the overriding coil with force. In a severe case the helmsman must bring the bow into the wind and take the strain off the working end of the sheet. The coil will then relax, releasing the tail.

When the sail fills on the new side and the sheet becomes tensioned, add one or two wraps to help secure the sheet to the winch. They will hold the sheet against the winch drum while the crew grinds with the winch handle. Once again the helmsman can make trimming easier by turning the bow toward the wind causing the jib to luff slightly while the crew grinds it home.

Some heavier cruising boats may resist tacking at slow speeds. These boats lose momentum and steerageway part way through the tack. Backwinding or delaying the release of the jib may be necessary to get the bow through the wind. Otherwise, you may be forced to jibe onto the other tack.

JIBING

After tacking, bear away and trim sails until you get to a broad reach; then prepare to jibe. Despite the apprehension often associated with jibing the main, it may be the preferred tactic as you bring the boat onto a run and sail wing and wing. Control of the boom is critical and the familiar method of centering it with the main sheet is the best choice. "Ready to jibe" and "jibing the main" should also be heard at the appropriate moments. When using the main sheet to center the boom be prepared to release it immediately as the sail fills on the new side. Sudden force in the mainsail could cause the boat to round-up.

Alert everyone to the possibility of accidentally jibing the main. Running wing and wing is a tenuous pursuit on any boat. Rig a preventer on the main boom. Concentrate on keeping the boat on a direct down-wind course. The consequences of wind shifts and poor helmsmanship have a less immediate effect on a large boat. The resulting jib collapse or main jibe also take longer to correct. Expect the larger boat to be slightly more forgiving, but less easily rehabilitated on a run.

When completing a jibe maneuver, avoid releasing the old working jib sheet until the jib fills on the new side. This helps keep the jib from blowing forward of the forestay.

Spending a few hours on a triangular or figure eight course is well worth the time and effort. Become familiar with just how quickly and efficiently the crew can control all maneuvers under sail. Fatigue becomes a factor in navigation. A course requiring multiple, quick tacks or jibes could become dangerous if the crew lacks stamina and teamwork. Knowing the crew's capabilities will help in planning the safest way to sail from point "A" to point "B".

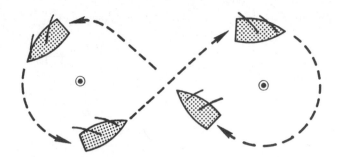

Figure eights using proper sail trim and tacking commands should be practiced to acquire a feel for the boat's maneuverability under sail.

THE COMPASS

You have already seen how compass directions apply to the chart. The binnacle compass gives the helmsman a reference for getting and keeping the boat moving in the intended direction. It consists of a compass card which displays numbers in a 360° circle beginning and ending with zero. Numbers appear in increments of 5 or 10 degrees. The compass card balances on a point at its center and is free to rotate. A magnet suspended beneath the card keeps the 0° or North mark pointing toward magnetic north. The lubber line, on the opposite side of the compass case from the helmsman, lines up with the bow. The number beside the lubber line indicates the boat's compass course. So the compass card does not really move. It always points north. The boat is attached to the binnacle on which the lubber line is marked and together they rotate beneath the compass card.

Most binnacle compasses have additional lubber lines offset by 45° or 90°. They allow you to steer without standing directly behind the compass by adding or subtracting the amount of the offset from your course.

The lubber line (1) on the binnacle compass rests beside the number that indicates the boat's magnetic heading.

SAILING A COMPASS COURSE

Draw an imaginary line from the center of the compass card, through the lubber line to the bow. When the boat turns, the bow and the lubber line both rotate. The bow travels a greater distance because it is further from the pivot point at the center of the compass card. The bow may move a few feet to one side or the other without the compass registering any significant difference. In fact, an inexperienced helmsman steering strictly by the compass can carve a winding path through the water and never even know it.

Jet skis and some other small boats may intentionally sail erratic courses just going here and there. Sailboats never do that. You should always be going in one direction unless you are altering your course to go in another direction.

One of the first challenges of basic sailing is to keep the boat on course; something you should already have mastered.

Now try it using only the compass. Get on a comfortable point of sail with plenty of sea room and landmark(s) in the distance. Notice your compass course. Next, eliminate the water and land from your field of view and look only at the compass. If wind and waves are present the boat will

Current can cause the boat's heading to differ considerably from the track it follows through the water.

provide the next part of the experiment. The compass will begin to drift and you must make adjustments with the helm to stay on course. After a few minutes, look back at your wake and see how well you did.

Try again, except this time split your viewing time between the compass and the land in the background. Looking over the bow gives you a much earlier indication of when and in which direction the boat will turn. Check the compass to make sure the overall course has not changed from your minor rudder adjustments.

Turn away from land and repeat the exercise. The absence of landmarks adds a degree of difficulty to steering a straight course; but you can usually tell if the bow is turning past the water's surface, the horizon or clouds in the sky. The masthead fly and telltales offer additional visual references. In fact, heavy fog and total darkness are the only times a helmsman must steer strictly by compass. Most experienced helmsmen look back and forth continuously between their surroundings and the compass.

A simple rule should help you steer while your compass steering senses develop. When the boat drifts off course, find the number on the compass card which indicates the desired course. If it lies to the right of the lubber line, turn the wheel to the right to get back on course. If it is to the left, turn the wheel to the left. Remembering this rule will help you avoid turning in the wrong direction and further confusing the situation.

Scan the horizon in a 360 arc every 10-15 minutes. Boats and ships can approach quickly and silently from any direction.

NAVIGATION RULES

The Navigation Rules were mentioned earlier in reference to sound signals in the fog. The official government publication (U. S. Coast Guard COMDTINST M16672.2 series) contains two sets of rules; international and inland. International Rules (known as COLREGS, short for International Regulations for Preventing Collisions at Sea, 1972) apply to the high seas and most foreign waters and waters up to U. S. lines of demarcation. These are lines on charts specifying the beginning of a harbor or bay. Demarcation lines for the entire country can be found in the back of the Navigation Rules. Inland Rules apply inside the demarcation lines.

Overall, the rules are similar for both international and inland. The following discussion touches on some highlights of rules 1-19 but you should study the official wording and complete treatment of the rules found in the Navigation Rules book. Students should buy a copy.

RULE 1
International Rules apply to all vessels on the high seas; and the Inland Rules apply to all vessels on the inland waters of the U. S. and to U. S. vessels on the Canadian waters of the Great Lakes as long as no conflict exists with Canadian law.

RULE 2
Nothing in the rules exonerates any vessel or its operators from the consequences of neglect to comply with the rules. However, there remains a possibility that special circumstances, Limitations of the vessel for example, could justify departure from the rules to avoid immediate danger.

RULE 3
These definitions are used in following the rules.

Vessel: Every description of watercraft.

Power driven vessel: Any vessel propelled by machinery

Sailing vessel: Any vessel under sail, provided propelling machinery (if fitted) is not being used.

Vessel engaged in fishing: Commercial fishing boats which are using apparatus which restrict their ability to maneuver.

Seaplane: Any aircraft designed to maneuver on the water.

Vessel not under command: A vessel that cannot maneuver according to the Rules due to some exceptional circumstances.

Vessel restricted in her ability to maneuver: A vessel which cannot maneuver according to the Rules because of the nature of her work.

Vessel constrained by her draft: A power driven vessel which, because of her draft in relation to the available depth of water, is unable to deviate from her course. (International Rules only)

Underway: A vessel which is not at anchor or made fast to the shore or ground.
Vessels are deemed to be in sight of one another only when one can be observed visually from the other.

Restricted visibility: Any condition including fog, mist, falling snow, heavy rainstorms and sandstorms which restrict visibility.

RULE 4
The Steering and Sailing Rules are divided into three subparts. The rules in the first subpart apply in any condition of visibility.

RULE 5
Every vessel, at all times, must maintain a proper look-out by sight and hearing as well as by all available means appropriate in the prevailing circumstances and conditions. The purpose of this lookout is to be able to make a full appraisal of the situation and the risk of collision. This rule has been interpreted to mean that someone other than the helmsman should be the lookout.

RULE 6
With respect to speed, the rules require every vessel to proceed at all times at a safe speed so it can take proper and effective action to avoid collisions and be stopped within a distance appropriate to the prevailing circumstances and conditions.

RULE 7

The rules require every vessel to use all available means appropriate to the prevailing circumstances and conditions to determine if risk of collision exists. If there is any doubt, such risk shall be deemed to exist. Radar, if fitted and working, must be used properly. Risk of collision should be deemed to exist if the compass bearing of an approaching vessel does not change appreciably.

RULE 8

Any action taken to avoid collision shall be positive, made in ample time and with due regard to the observance of good seamanship. The rules also mention that an alteration of course or speed shall be large enough to be readily apparent to another vessel. Cruising sailors often have an opportunity to exaggerate their intended response to a situation and,

thereby, inform an approaching vessel of what she may expect. The rule also says that a vessel should take all way off by operating astern propulsion to avoid collision or to get more time to assess the danger in a situation.

Two vessels, whose bearing (angle) relative to one another remains constant as their courses converge, are probably on a collision course.

No vessel should anchor in a narrow channel. The rules specify signals that must be sounded when vessels overtake one another in a channel. The Inland Rules also state that in certain river waters the downbound vessel, with a following current, has the right-of-way.

RULE 9

A vessel proceeding along the course of a narrow channel or fairway must keep as near to the outer limit of the channel or fairway which lies on her starboard side as is safe and practicable.
Also, a vessel less than 20 meters in length or a sailing vessel, regardless of its size, shall not impede the passage of a vessel that can safely navigate only within a channel.

Rule 10

Areas heavily traveled by commercial traffic often have designated shipping lanes. Vessels traveling away from a commercial harbor are supposed to use one lane and traffic moving toward the harbor uses another. Together, the lanes and the Traffic Separation Zone, usually a mile or more in width, are called the Traffic Separation Scheme.

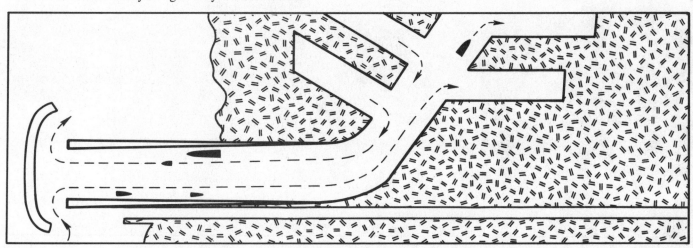

Prescribed traffic patterns should be observed at all times.

The International Rules have a few key points which frequently apply to sailors. The chart clearly indicates which direction each lane flows. Vessels traveling in the lane should enter at the smallest angle possible, that is by traveling nearly parallel to the lane. Pleasure boats should travel outside shipping lanes. The separation zone is restricted to navigation. It may be entered only to cross. Boats should always enter the separation scheme at right angles and cross as quickly as possible.

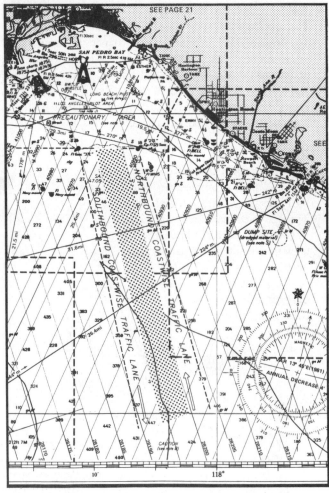

Traffic separation zones are clearly indicated on NOAA charts.

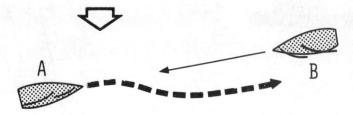

(A) alters course in plenty of time to avoid a collision with (B).

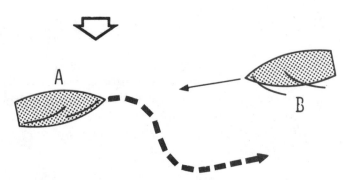

A give-way vessel (A) exaggerates its course to make its intentions clear to (B) the stand-on vessel.

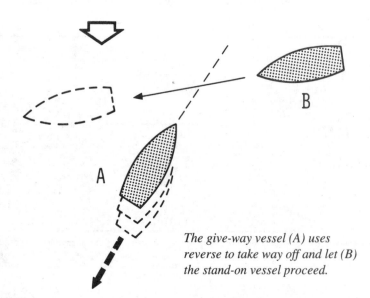

The give-way vessel (A) uses reverse to take way off and let (B) the stand-on vessel proceed.

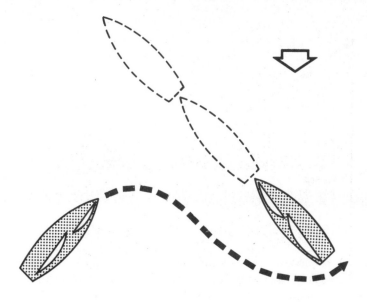

The starboard tack vessel is the stands-on while the port tack vessel gives-way, altering course to avoid collision.

The rule above applies regardless of point of sail.

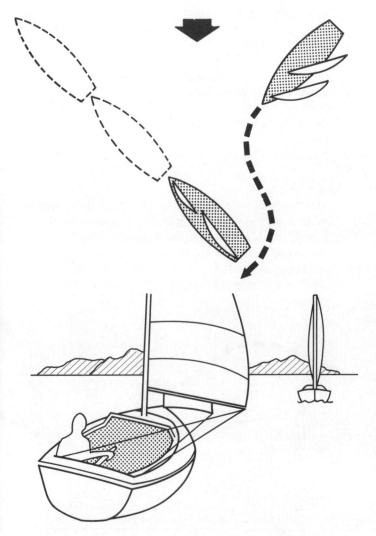

The foreground boat should avoid the approaching vessel because the other boat's rights are not evident.

The Inland Rules simply require vessels to comply with the applicable vessel traffic service regulations.

RULE 11

The second subpart of the steering and sailing rules only applies to vessels in sight of one another.

RULE 12

The rules for sailboats are the same as those you learned for smaller boats.

• When two sailboats approach on opposite tacks the boat on port tack shall keep out of the way of the other boat.

• When both boats are on the same tack the windward boat shall keep out of the way of the leeward boat.

• A vessel on port tack that sees an approaching boat whose tack is unknown shall keep out of the way of the other boat.

The three situations in which two boats can collide are overtaking, crossing and meeting. Overtaking occurs when one vessel approaches another from astern, on either side within the area aft of a point 22.5° abaft the beam. If you drew a line through the beam perpendicular to the center line and measured out 22.5° further aft, the lines drawn outward through that point on both sides would mark the overtaking sector. This coincides with the area in which a vessel's stern light is visible. The crossing sector occupies everything forward of those lines except when two boats approach each other bow to bow, which is called meeting.

RULE 13

Any vessel, whether sail or power, overtaking any other shall keep out of the way of the vessel being overtaken.

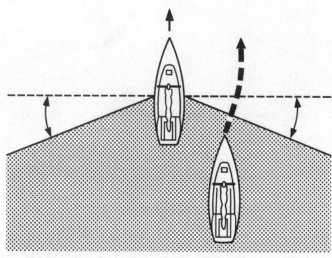

A boat approaching another vessel in the shaded area (between 22.5° aft of the beam on either side) is overtaking.

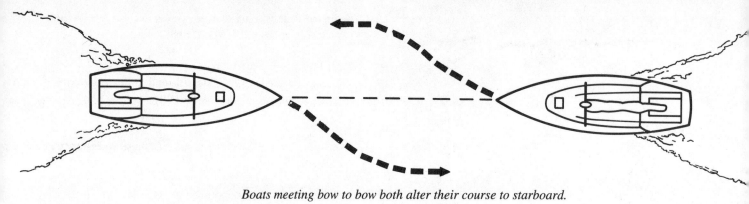

Boats meeting bow to bow both alter their course to starboard.

RULE 14

When two power driven vessels are meeting on reciprocal or nearly reciprocal courses so as to involve risk of collision, each shall alter her course to starboard so that each shall pass on the port side of the other. (fig 2-26)

RULE 15

When two power driven vessels are crossing, the vessel which has the other on her starboard side shall keep out of the way and shall avoid crossing ahead of the other vessel. The Inland Rules add that on certain river waters a vessel crossing a river shall keep out of the way of power driven vessels ascending or descending the river.

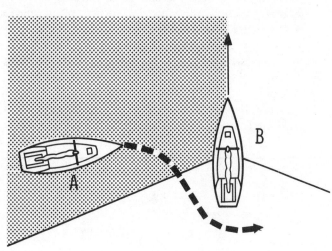

Vessels approaching from the shaded area and the corresponding area on (B)'s starboard side are crossing. (A) gives way to (B) according to Rule 15.

RULE 16

Whenever one vessel must stay out of the way of another it is called the Give-way vessel. It must always take early and substantial action to keep well clear.

RULE 17

The vessel that is not directed to stay out of the way is called the Stand-on vessel and she must keep her course and speed in a situation where these rules come into play. The rule goes on to say that the Stand-on vessel may take

action to avoid collision if the Give-way vessel fails to take appropriate action, and she is required to act to avoid a collision when the Give-way vessel is so close it cannot avoid collision by itself.

RULE 18

A "pecking order" exists within the various types of vessels defined earlier. Each vessel must stay out of the way of all other vessels that appear higher on the list.

Not under command
Restricted in ability to maneuver
(the first two are of equal precedence)
Constrained by draft (does not apply to Inland Rules)
Fishing
Sail
Power
Seaplane

RULE 19

The third subpart of the Steering and Sailing Rules applies in restricted visibility. The rules here require a vessel to proceed at a safe speed adapted to the prevailing circumstances and conditions. If a fog signal is heard, apparently forward of the beam, a vessel must reduce speed to bare steerageway and proceed with extreme caution.

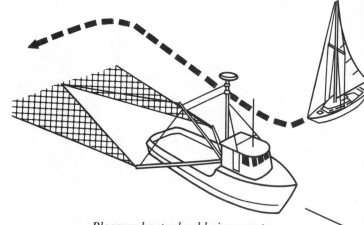

Pleasure boats should give-way to commercial fishing vessels engaged in fishing.

MAN OVERBOARD

In the days when wooden ships transported brave and hearty men across oceans for trade and exploration, loss of crew members ranked with scurvy and spoiled provisions as a bitter punishment for trespassing in Poseidon's kingdom. Crewmen traversed slippery decks, climbed rigging and balanced on yards a hundred feet above deck in the worst conditions. When they were swept overboard they were almost certainly gone for good.

Today we rarely need to climb the mast. Decks and deck shoes reduce slipping. Sailors in many modern sailboats hardly ever leave the cockpit. Sailing technology has changed tremendously since the days of old, but the deadly consequences of accidentally falling overboard have not. The best defense against the dangers of an accidental dunking is to prevent it from happening in the first place. Understand the importance of keeping "one hand for you and one hand for the boat". The crew should wear some type of PFD while on deck in all but the most benign conditions. An increasing number of boaters wear personal inflatable PFDs at all times. They are lighter and more comfortable than a Type I, II or III.

Using a safety harness significantly reduces the chances of falling overboard. The harness fits snugly around the rib cage. It attaches a person to the boat with a tether, a line which can quickly clip or unclip to a secure point on the boat. Some boat owners mount pad eyes in places where crew members are apt to spend a great deal of time or be particularly vulnerable. The cockpit sole near the helm and close to the mast are two examples. Shrouds are acceptable, too, but lifelines are not.

Jack lines are strong lines that extend from bow to stern on both sides of the boat between deck cleats. The tether's usual 6 to 8 foot length allows someone to clip on to the jack line and work at nearly any spot on the boat.

MAN OVERBOARD RECOVERY

Sailors wince at many sounds aboard ship. Any bang, boom or pop could require emergency procedures or unwelcome repair work. The single most dreaded sound on a sailboat is another crew member's voice yelling "man overboard".

Unfortunately, conditions develop that catch someone unprepared and the boat sails off without one of its crew. The actions taken immediately by the remaining sailors make the difference between an amusing sea story and a regrettable disaster.

The ASA recommends a figure eight recovery technique in its Basic Keelboat Sailing standard. There are other ways of getting back to someone in the water; but this method has proven to be effective, easily executed and safe. The following steps will take you through a figure eight man overboard recovery.

1. **Alert the crew by yelling "man overboard".**

2. **Throw a type IV PFD or any other instantly available floatation.** Some authorities on the subject recommend throwing a number of things that float. Other life preservers and fenders are examples. More floatation will help keep the victim afloat and leave a visual trail back to the person.

3. **Designate a pointer.** Give someone the job of keeping an eye on the victim and pointing to him or her. That person should keep repeating where the person is in relation to the boat. For example, "two boat lengths directly off the stern", etc.

4. **Put the boat on a beam reach.** Regardless of what point of sail the boat was on when the person fell overboard, the helmsman should get the boat sailing immediately on a beam reach and note the course. You will always be able to sail a reciprocal course to the area where the victim fell from the boat when you sail away on a beam reach.

5. **Sail away from the victim.** This is the most difficult and dangerous part of this technique. Getting the victim onboard the first time is a very high priority. The helmsman needs some distance to correctly execute the next steps. The crew needs time to prepare to get the person back aboard. Sail the boat no more than ten boat lengths away.

6. **Come about.** Tacking is far more controllable and organized than jibing. It will keep the crew focused and minimize the panic onboard.

7. **Release the jib sheet.** Let the jib luff immediately after the tack. The boat will begin to slow down.

8. **Sail back to the victim.** The helmsman should head for a spot about four or five boat lengths from the victim and slightly down wind. Get to a position that will allow the boat to travel the remaining distance on a close reach. Close reaching allows the main to luff and the boat to slow down or power back up if it falls short of the person in the water.

9. **Line up on a close reach and luff the main.** The boat does not slow down until the main luffs completely. The distance a boat needs to slow down and stop beside a person in the water will vary according to boats and conditions. Practice in various conditions and always on an unfamiliar boat. The boat must be nearly stopped for the crew to offer adequate assistance.

10. **Stop beside the victim.** The helmsman must use some judgment when deciding whether to come to windward or leeward of the victim. In treacherous conditions stopping to windward and near the victim could cause the boat to be lifted by waves and dropped on the person in the water. In less severe conditions the boat could provide shelter from wind and wave. The ASA Basic Keelboat Sailing text recommends stopping to windward and throwing a line to the person in the water. The appropriate actions at this point will vary with the situation.

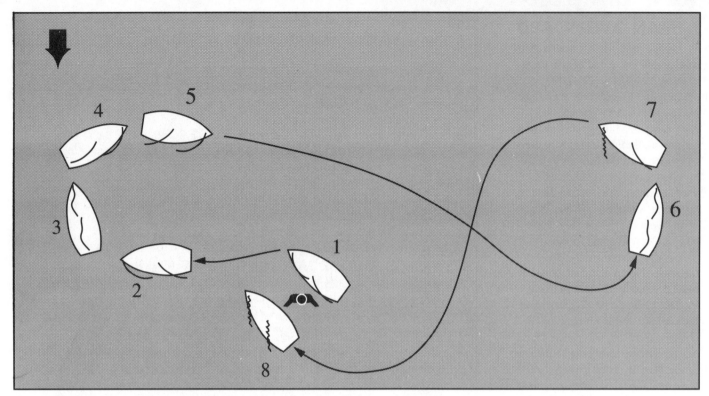

Figure 8 man overboard recovery (1) Victim falls overboard, (2) boat goes onto a beam reach, (3) heading-up, (4) tacking, (5) bearing away and sailing back on a beam reach, (6) heading -up, (7) tacking, release jib sheet, bear ing away, (8) line-up for a close reach approach, release mainsail, slow boat and retrieve victim.

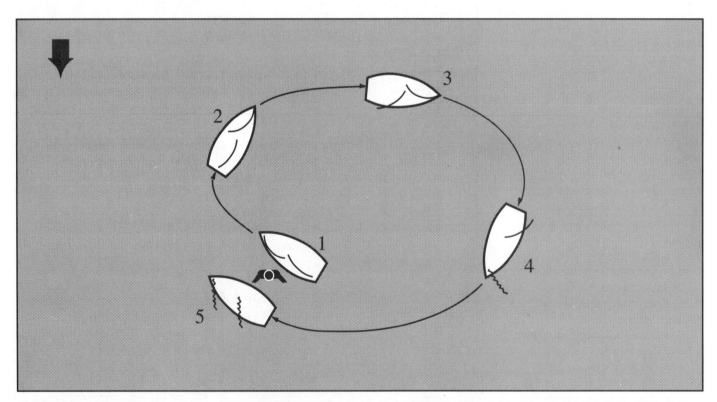

Quick stop man overboard recovery   (1) Victim falls overboard, (2) heading-up, tack without releasing the jib sheet, (3) bearing away, (4) jibing, lining up slightly downwind of the victim, luffing sails, (5) return to the victim on a close reach with sails luffing.

RETRIEVING A MAN OVERBOARD

Returning to a person in the water begins the process of a safe return to the vessel. What you do when the boat and swimmer are reunited can be just as critical to success as promptly returning to the victim's location. Problems rarely occur in calm, pleasant conditions. Some combination of strong wind and high seas usually help sweep someone off the deck. Those same conditions will interfere with the recovery process.

As the boat slows down near the person in the water its maneuverability becomes limited. You should assume that you have less than a minute to keep the boat and person together. A line with a bowline large enough to slip easily around the person's body will help secure the person to the boat. The Lifesling® uses a length of line with a floating, bright yellow harness at the end. By trailing it from the stern and circling the victim using the Quick Stop recovery method, it will eventually pass the swimmer's location. It slips over the body and he or she is pulled to the boat.

If you were forced to use the motor, it should be turned off (not simply put in neutral) by the time you get to a position beside the person in the water. As mentioned, a spinning propeller and the swimmer should be kept from one another. Never place a line in the water with the propeller in motion. The Lifesling® and its line floats, but its line could become a problem if it were forced under the boat.

Once the person is secured to the boat you have a number of options for getting him or her back aboard. In the best of situations the person can climb back aboard with the helping hands of a few crew members. Lack of consciousness or strength could force you to select another method. Resist the temptation to put someone in the water to help the victim unless it is absolutely the only solution. Then the helper must wear a PFD, a harness and be secured to the boat with a strong tether.

THE QUICK STOP METHOD

Critics complain that the figure eight method requires the boat to travel a considerable distance from the victim's location. The time and distance involved increase the chances of losing sight of the person. A less traditional technique called the quick stop method keeps the boat and victim closer together.

1. **Follow steps one and two from the figure eight method.**

2. **Tack immediately, but do not release the jib.** Backwinding it slows the boat down and forces it to turn faster.

3. **Bear away.** **Continue turning, trimming the main as you go.**

4. **Jibe.**

5. **Release or drop the jib.**

6. **Return to the victim on a close reach.**

7. **Luff the main and retrieve the victim.**

If the first attempt fails, then the process should be repeated turning the boat in tight circles until the victim is back on board. Practice with every new boat. The procedure may be difficult with some designs.

Make sure your attempts to save someone never injure them further. Here are a few things to remember:

- Never sail so close that you hit the victim with the boat. It often takes expert helmsmanship but you must get close enough to assist without running the person over.

- Avoid using the engine. It may seem like the most reliable way to get directly to your victim, but a spinning propeller and a swimmer do not mix well. Practice sailing man overboard recoveries enough to feel confident using only sail power.

- If your boat has a LORAN or GPS receiver, instruct several crew members on the way to record the boat's present position in the set's memory. They should be told to record the position as they come topside in response to a "man overboard" report. This can be valuable information if you lose sight of the victim while maneuvering.

- Never react so quickly that your crew members are in danger of being injured or thrown into the water themselves. Larger boats require more hands. Take an extra moment to explain your strategy. An unassisted, kamikaze style tack or jibe can only worsen an already critical situation.

USING AVAILABLE EQUIPMENT

If the boom has a bale or other fitting near the aft end it could be used to support a person's weight. Lead the line that has been tied around the victim through the bale or attach an appropriate sized block to the bale and run the line through it. A deck winch in the mast area could provide the necessary pulling power. A cockpit winch might also do the trick. This winch may tend to pull the boom inboard and will require a few strong crew to hold the boom away from the boat. Placing a fairlead block on the toe rail helps redirect the force.

An easily removable boom vang could offer another solution. Attach it to the bale. The built-in mechanical advantage might eliminate the need for a winch.

A halyard with a long tail might also work. Determine in advance whether leading it outboard will cause it to jump a sheave at the masthead. Halyards are generally intended to run only fore and aft.

Check the integrity of the topping lift if your plans call for using the boom to lift a heavy weight. The sail will hold a tremendous amount of weight but in any wind the boom becomes very difficult to control if the mainsail remains hoisted. Topping lifts are usually intended only to support the weight of the boom and it could be a weak link in your lifting plans. A halyard clipped to the end of the boom can eliminate any doubts.

USING THE DINGHY

A person without adequate strength to climb onto the boat may be able to negotiate the shallower freeboard on a dinghy. Climbing over the transom of the boat from a standing position in the dinghy requires far less strength than pulling one's entire body weight out of the water.

Placing a person's entire weight on the dinghy's gunnels or transom can create a different set of problems. A hard dinghy can easily capsize under the weight of a swimmer. Inflatables can withstand more weight but capsizing is not out of the question.

Another crew member can get into the dinghy and act as a counterweight. Sitting in the bow can balance the effects of the other person climbing over the transom.

Once the victim has been recovered treatment for shock, hypothermia or other physical injuries may be necessary. Do not let the person shrug off the experience and resume normal duties. Require a period of at least 8 hours for rest, recuperation and observation before standing watches or working again.

A 4 to 1 purchase block and tackle boom vang attached to the end of the boom can help a smaller person retrieve a larger person from the water.

The dinghy can offer a short intermediate step for getting a person from the water to the boat.

USING THE VHF

The VHF radio was introduced in Section I. Monitoring the local weather channel should be an important part of your pre-sail check list. The VHF also plays other vital roles in the crew's and boat's safety.

Channel options vary on VHF radios according to manufacturer and model. Most radios have at least one of the most important types of channels. For example, even the least sophisticated VHF will have one weather channel, one emergency channel, one ship to ship channel and one marine operator channel. The following is a list of the available channels and their designated uses.

CHANNEL 16

Most commercial and pleasure vessels monitor channel 16 unless some other arrangements have been made. Law enforcement agencies including the Coast Guard can be reached on 16. It is reserved for emergencies and hailing. Never conduct any other business on channel 16. The Coast Guard will interrupt any non-essential communications. If you hail a vessel on channel 16, the first thing you discuss with them is what ship to ship channel both boats can communicate on. Even in an emergency the Coast Guard radio operator will instruct the vessel calling to switch to a working channel.

EMERGENCY TRANSMISSIONS

There are three categories of urgent VHF broadcasts. "Mayday" indicates that a loss of vessel or life is imminent. Never send a "Mayday" unless the situation is that severe. Law enforcement officials take these calls very seriously.

"Pan -pan" (pronounced pon - pon) means the transmitting station has an urgent message concerning the safety of a vessel or person. "Securite" (pronounced say-curatay) preceeds a message concerning navigation safety or weather. If some large floating object was blocking a harbor entrance or an isolated weather hazard was moving through an area the warning would be broadcast as a "securite".

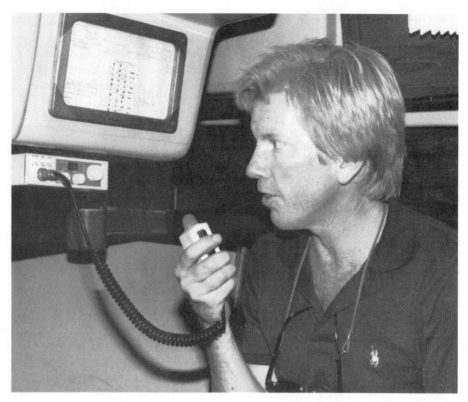

Speak clearly into the microphone and avoid yelling.

VHF CHANNELS FOR U. S. RADIO USERS

Distress, Safety and Calling 16

Intership Safety 6

Coast Guard Communications 22A

Port Operations...........................1, 5, 65A, 66A, 12, 73, 14, 74, 63, 20, 77
(intership and ship to coast)

Navigational 13, 67
(intership and ship to coast)

Non-commercial...68, 9, 69, 71, 78A, 72
(intership and ship to coast)

Non-commercial...72
(intership)

Commercial 1, 7A, 9, 10, 18A, 19A, 79A, 80A, 63
(commercial intership and ship to coast only)

Commercial 67, 8, 77, 88A
(commercial intership only)

Public Correspondence 24, 84, 25, 85, 26, 86, 27, 87, 28
(ship to coast marine operator)

SHIP TO SHIP

Communications between ships often provide valuable safety information. With the exception of the urgent broadcasts described above, the FCC regards the communications originating from VHF radios as point to point communications. Your radio calls should be directed to one receiver only. When you call another boat it should be hailed by name. Follow these steps to hail another vessel.

1. **Turn the radio on and select the channel.**

2. **Adjust the squelch and set the volume at about half way.**

3. **Set the power at 1 watt if the other vessel is nearby and 25 watts otherwise.**

4. **Listen for other traffic on the channel and wait until it is clear.**

5. **Depress the button on the microphone and speak clearly.** Hail the other vessel three times; identify yourself, say "over", then release the button and listen for a reply. For example, "Adventurer, Adventurer, Adventurer, this is Capricious Whisky Yankee Echo 2214, over". "Whiskey, Yankee and Echo are the phonetic alphabet words (see accompanying chart) for the three letter prefix of the boat's radio call sign. These letters and numbers are assigned by the FCC when they issue a license. Post it on or near the radio.

6. **Wait 2 minutes before repeating the process.** After three attempts, wait and try again later.

When the other vessel responds, switch to the mutually agreed working channel; then conduct your business as efficiently and quickly as possible. Always say "over" when you have finished speaking and await an answer.

7. Sign off by restating your call letters and saying "out". "This is Whiskey, Yankee, Echo 2214 out." Or you may say, "Clear with Adventurer, standing by on one six" (channel 16).

RADIO CHECK

Determine whether your VHF can transmit and receive by conducting a radio check. Ideally the radio check occurs between your vessel and a particular other boat. Select an appropriate ship to ship channel. Listen for traffic and when it is clear, send your message. "Adventurer, Adventurer, Adventurer this is Capricious Whiskey, Yankee, Echo 2214 for a radio check, over."

The other boat answers and you sign off as you would on any other call.

We cannot always find a familiar fellow boater to help with the radio check. Sailors often disregard the point to point nature of the VHF and ask, "Any vessel for a radio check". The usual response is "Loud and clear in (location)". The practice is very common and apparently the FCC turns a deaf ear in the interest of boating safety.

YOU WOULD BROADCAST AN URGENT MESSAGE IN THE FOLLOWING MANNER:

- "MAYDAY, MAYDAY, MAYDAY"

- "THIS IS   (your boat name)
  (your boat name)
  (your boat name)
  (your call sign)"

- "MAYDAY (your boat name)"

- "POSITION IS:
  (your vessel's position in degrees and minutes of latitude and longitude or in nautical miles from and bearing to a navigational landmark)"

- (state the type of emergency)

- "WE REQUIRE:
  (the type of assistance you seek)"

  (the number of adults and children aboard)

  (your boat name, its length in feet, type of boat and its color and markings)

- "WE ARE STANDING BY ON CHANNEL 16"

- "THIS IS
  (your boat name and call sign)"

- "OVER"

Coast Guard receivers and transmitters are usually the most powerful radios in their areas. Occasionally, a boater will hear a "Mayday" which cannot be heard by the Coast Guard. If the "Mayday" broadcast continues unanswered, you can respond. Then contact the Coast Guard on behalf of the distressed vessel by following the method above except you call it "Mayday relay" and identify your vessel and call sign.

Either as the distressed vessel or a relay, you will be asked some very specific questions by the Coast Guard operator. You will also be given very specific directions. Pay very close attention and avoid appointing anyone even slightly hysterical to call the Coast Guard. The moments following a "Mayday" call are usually critical.

THE PHONETIC ALPHABET

A—Alpha	J—Juliet	S—Sierra
B—Bravo	K—Kilo	T—Tango
C—Charlie	L—Lima	U—Uniform
D—Delta	M—Mike	V—Victor
E—Echo	N—November	W—Whiskey
F—Foxtrot	O—Oscar	X—X-ray
G—Golf	P—Papa	Y—Yankee
H—Hotel	Q—Quebec	Z—Zulu
I—India	R—Romeo	

MARINE OPERATOR

The channels indicated as "Public Correspondence" in the preceding chart above are reserved for telephone transmissions. People on land can contact any ship with a VHF monitoring the appropriate channel and within range. Simply dial the operator and ask for the marine operator. Supply the name of the vessel and the marine operator will hail it on his or her assigned channel as well as channel 16.

You may connect with a marine operator to place a call from a vessel by following these steps.

1. **Find the public marine operator channel.** It is usually found between 24 or 27. A marine electronics dealer or another experienced boater could supply local information. Listen for other traffic on those channels.

2. **Hail the operator.** "Miami marine, Miami marine, Miami marine this is Capricious, Whiskey, Yankee, Echo 2214 over." Repeat as you would a ship to ship call.

3. **Wait for a reply.** You will be given instructions. Calling rates are very high, so be brief. You may pay by reversing the charges, charging it to your home phone or to a credit card. Your credit card number, along with everything else you say, will be heard by everyone who happens to be listening so you may want to be discrete.

UNLOCKING THE CHART'S SECRETS

Every bit of information on a chart has meaning and significance. Most chart symbols represent actual objects on the water or land. Begin using the chart to your advantage by locating charted objects in your local sailing area. Buoys, day beacons, radio towers and light houses are examples of some easily located objects which appear on the chart.

Most buoys have markings with numbers or letters. When many buoys of the same shape and color appear in one area the numbers and letters take on added importance. Remember the saying, "red, right, returning". It means that on the way into a harbor or up a channel the red buoys and day beacons are located to the right. Green aids to navigation are on the left. Unlighted red buoys marking a channel are tapered at the top and are called nuns. Unlighted green buoys are cylindrical and called cans. Lighted buoys are an exception to the shape rule.

Green day beacons are square and red day beacons are triangular. Green navigation aids are odd numbered and red aids are even numbered. The lowest numbers begin at the entrance and increase as they ascend the channel. Chart No. 1, a government publication, lists all chart symbols. It gives important information on the symbols and it should be onboard every boat.

The chart translates the characteristics of its environment into a two dimensional representation. While charts are invaluable navigating tools they lack the ability to represent the visual qualities of land and water. For example, the chart can provide the shape of an island quite accurately. On approach to the island, however, you are apt to see only a land mass ahead. The protruding points of land and the distinctly receding bays are often not visible when viewed from sea level. Coast Pilot, another government publication, provides descriptions of landfalls and other valuable information for mariners. It should be onboard any vessel that cruises into unfamiliar waters.

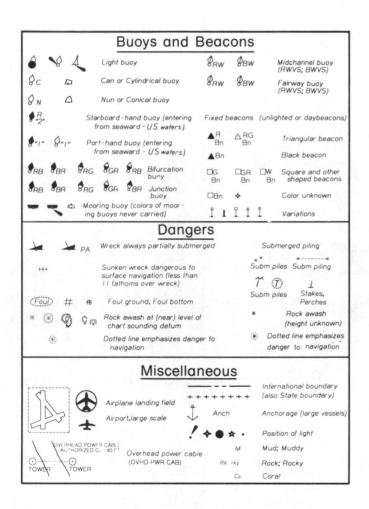

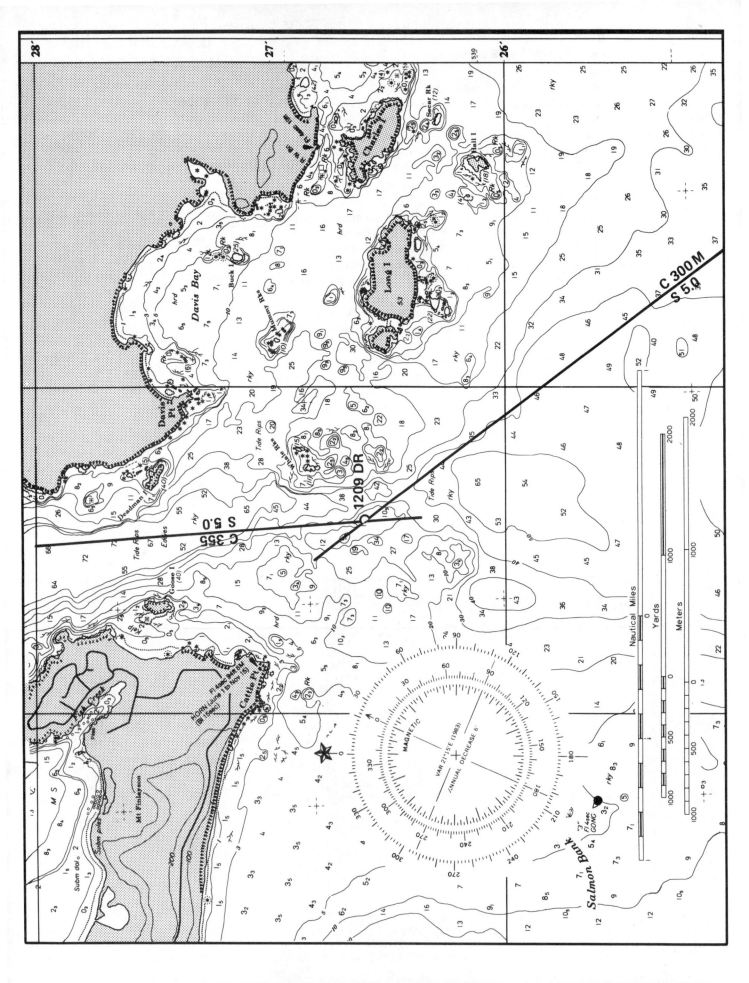

DEAD RECKONING

Your introduction to the nautical chart in section II required that you lay off a course. The track you laid out is your intended course, not necessarily your actual course through the water. Leeway, the tendency for the boat to move sideways through the water, will occur because of the keel and rudder's inability to totally resist lateral motion. Current, wind or waves can also place the boat in a position quite different from where you thought it would be.

Applying the speed, time and distance information from the previous section to your course line is known as dead reckoning or DR. The term has evolved slightly since the Portuguese explorers introduced the practice centuries ago. It was originally called "deduced reckoning" then shortened to "ded reckoning" before it became "dead reckoning".

Any time you can pinpoint the boat's location on a chart with reasonable accuracy you have a fix. A fix appears on a chart as a circle with a dot in the middle. Beside it and perpendicular to the course line indicate the time (24 hour military style). You should always fix your position at the beginning of a journey. You know enough to consider it a fix because you can see the first sea buoy or harbor entrance. This fix also allows you to begin your dead reckoning.

Once the boat speed has been established your dead reckoning can begin. Select logical intervals of time to update your dead reckoning. Every half hour or hour may work depending on the distance of your voyage and the proximity of land and obstructions. A long trip across deep, open water would not benefit by frequent chart updates unless the speed or course changes.

You can use the 60D=ST equation to find the distance traveled between periodic chart updates. For example, if your speed is 5 knots and you choose to update your DR every 30 minutes the equation would be 60D=5 x 30 or D=2.5. Measure the distance on the latitude scale. Label your dead reckoning positions with a half circle and a dot. The time should appear similar to a fix. Update your DR whenever the boat changes course or speed regardless of the time.

These two publications should be on board every cruising sailboat.

DEVIATION

As mentioned earlier, 000° on the compass card should always point to magnetic north. The magnetic ability built into the compass card aligns it with the earth's strong magnetic field. Magnetic fields on the boat can interfere with this continuous attraction and alter the position of the compass card.

Anything with its own magnetic field can deflect the position of the compass. Every radio speaker has a magnet. Experiment by taking a portable radio and passing it around the binnacle compass. The card follows the radio as it passes. Large, ferrous metal objects can have the same effect. The engine block might exert some magnetic influence on the compass card.

Boat owners often have professionals "swing" their compass. They use an azimuth circle to determine the boat's heading compared to the known direction of the sun. They record the difference between the binnacle compass reading and the calculated heading. After correcting for variation, any difference is called deviation and it becomes an important factor for navigation.

A thorough treatment of deviation lies beyond the scope of this text, but its adverse effects can be eliminated by double checking the binnacle compass with a hand bearing compass.

A hand bearing compass indicates the bearing to an object or the magnetic direction of a line from you to another object.

It works exactly like a binnacle compass except it can go where you go. Practice by sighting objects on shore or other boats through the hand bearing compass. Pause a moment after moving it to allow the card to stabilize in one position. The boat's motion also makes precise readings a challenge.

Determine the boat's compass deviation by following these steps.

1. **Use the binnacle compass to get the boat on the desired compass course.**

2. **Place a crew member somewhere away from strong magnetic fields.** Forward of the mast or all the way aft are usually good choices. He or

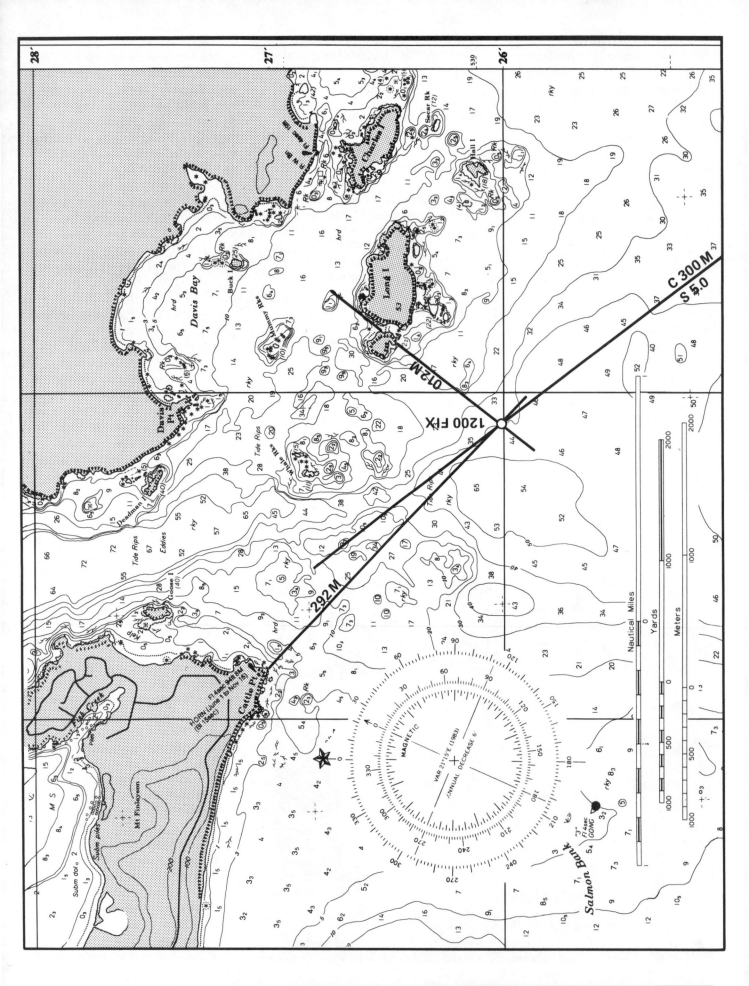

she should start at the center line of the boat and sight directly forward.

3. **Crew member and helmsman call out numbers and compare headings until a pattern surfaces.** The headings may be the same or they may differ by a constant number of degrees. The difference should be consistent through the few degrees of course change caused by wind and waves.

4. **Alter course until the hand bearing compass indicates you are on the desired course.** Note the new binnacle course and steer that course. Recheck periodically and always after a course change because deviation changes when a boat changes course.

PLOTTING A FIX

Whenever the boat's course brings it near land the opportunity may exist to get a fix. The probability of DR inaccuracy increases with time and distance. Plotting a fix gives you an opportunity to lay off a new course to your destination in the event your fix disagrees with the DR position. You can also double check your speed.

A two or three bearing fix can be accomplished easily by two crew members.

1. **Locate two or, preferably, three objects which can be seen clearly from the deck and also appear on the chart.** Avoid floating navigation aids if possible because they tend to move from their charted location.

2. **Station one person on deck with the hand bearing compass.** Position that person amidships to reduce effects of the boat's motion. Station the other person below at the chart table.

3. **Practice sighting the objects a few times in fairly rapid succession.** Notice whether the bearings are consistent and how long it takes the compass to settle down after moving from one to another.

4. **The person on deck calls out each object and its bearing.** For instance, "water tower 135, lighthouse 170, corner of the south jetty 200".

5. **The person below records the bearings and objects in a log book along with the time.** The sightings should all be complete within 30 seconds.

6. **Plot the bearings.** Begin at the magnetic compass rose. Align the parallel rules with the appropriate magnetic bearing and the cross in the center. Walk them to the corresponding object. Draw a line from the object to the vicinity of your DR position. Do the same for each object. The place where the lines meet is your fix. Label it as a fix with the time. Calculate the revised source to your destination and start a new DR plot from the fix.

Your accuracy with the hand bearing compass will improve with practice. Select objects whose angles to one another at the time of the fix are not too small or too large. Three objects that are 60° apart are ideal.

Careful sighting through a hand bearing compass can help add accuracy to your navigation.

CONCLUSION

Sailing a larger boat on longer voyages adds a whole new set of skills to your existing collection. A higher caliber, more responsible mariner eagerly replaces the relatively carefree day sailor. A new set of tools makes the discharge of these new responsibilities more manageable. And, while learning new rules, procedures and equipment can become tiring, remember that responsibility begets privilege. You are gaining clearance to new and fascinating places. The beauty and intrigue that await cruising sailors are the things that make dreams and legends. A new and exciting world will unfold at the other end of every new chart.

ARRIVAL & LIVING ABOARD

"We arrived at the island just at sunset. It was too dark to see the bottom in order to find a clear place, and it is necessary to be very careful in order not to lose the anchors. The beaches are all clear, without boulders, but there are some rocks underwater near the shore, and you must keep your eyes peeled when you wish to anchor and not anchor too near shore. The water is very clear and you can see the bottom during the daylight hours, but a couple of lombard shots (600 yards) offshore there is so much depth that you cannot find bottom."

—The Log of Christopher Columbus—

The incredible variety in any sailing adventure makes cruising an activity that offers something for everyone. Handy crew members enjoy tinkering in the boat's mechanical quarters. Navigation, the challenge of predicting and fixing the boat's position, captures the attention of those who find pleasure in solving mathematical mysteries. Cooks perform miracles in the galley, orderly sailors tidy up and everyone enjoys the enchanting simplicity of the boat moving through the crystal blue water, propelled by successfully harnessing nature's forces.

As a spectacular bonus, some of the world's most charming, picturesque and fascinating places lie at the end of each day's journey. Every year thousands of modern-day seafarers swim, snorkel, windsurf and explore exotic new shores using an anchored sailboat as their temporary floating home. If getting there is half the fun, being there is certainly the other half. This section provides readers with the skills to arrive safely and enjoy life at their chosen anchorages.

RIGHTS IN ANCHORAGES

Every boat has the right to lie at anchor without collision. Boats arriving at an anchorage must position themselves well clear of other anchored vessels. Determine the anchoring method other boats in the anchorage have used. You should either use the same method or anchor well clear of neighboring boats.

A boat anchored by its bow can swing in a 360° circle. The diameter of that circle can be nearly double the length of the boat's anchor rode. 50 yards of rode creates the need for a 100 yard diameter circle of swinging room. A neighboring boat must anchor far enough away to ensure that the circle created by his swinging boat does not intersect the circle created by any other boat swinging around its anchor. Anchoring "bow only" generally requires the most distance between boats.

Boats anchoring in a moderate breeze often take a chance and anchor within another boat's swinging circle. As long as the breeze blows steadily or shifts only through a small angle, each boat points into the wind at the end of a taut anchor rode. They will not collide while anchored in roughly the same water depth with the same rode length. Problems arise when the wind quits. Anchored boats tend to drift in random patterns. If two boats' swinging circles intersect, they stand a good chance of colliding when the steady wind is replaced by lulls, variable puffs and current eddies.

Boats use various methods to reduce their swinging radii. (see Sailing Skills) A new arrival must determine if other boats are using these techniques. Anchor in a way that will reduce swing if the earlier arrivals have chosen to do so. Otherwise, select an anchorage far enough away from the other boats to keep you from fouling them regardless of wind direction.

Boating people tend to be friendly and cooperative. Motor slowly past other boats prior to anchoring. People on deck will usually tell you about depth, holding ground and obstructions. Inquire about their rode length and ask how the wind acted if they have been there overnight. They may have had swimmers in the area who can report on uncharted obstructions. Use this knowledge with the information on the chart and in the cruising guide. Always give other boats in the anchorage plenty of room regardless of anchoring technique. They probably wouldn't be there if they wanted neighbors a boat length or so away.

INTERNATIONAL TRAVEL

Sailboat cruising may bring boat and crew across international borders. Great Lakes sailors pass between U. S. and Canadian waters. Both Britain and the U.S. own territory in the Virgin Islands. Travel between U. S. and British islands requires crossing an international border despite the islands' close proximity.

Research the area where you will enter another country or re-enter the country of origin. Locate the nearest Port of Entry. You must check in with customs and usually immigrations immediately upon entering a country. If you enter at a port without a customs office, the ship and crew are quarantined until customs arrives to check the boat in. Only the skipper may be allowed to visit the local Port Captain or other law enforcement official to arrange a visit by customs. Customs agents usually consider traveling to a remote harbor an inconvenience. You may wait a long time for clearance and pay substantial additional fees. Clear in through a normal Port of Entry whenever possible.

Tie up to the customs dock. The skipper must gather the ship's documents as well as those of the entire crew and report directly to the customs office. Your prior research will reveal what personal documents are necessary. In some cases it might be just a driver's license, but other jurisdictions may require a passport or a passport and a visa. Some customs officials may impose mild decorum; all will appreciate courtesy and patience. Show respect by wearing a shirt and shoes into the building.

Pacific Region 20
San Diego District:
Port of Entry: San Diego.
Los Angeles District:
Ports of Entry: Los Angeles-Long Beach, Port San Luis. 25

Customs Station: Port Hueneme.
San Francisco District:
Ports of Entry: San Francisco-Oakland, Eureka.
Customs Station: Monterey.
Columbia-Snake (at Portland) District: 30
Ports of Entry: Astoria, Coos Bay, Longview, Newport.

Seattle District:
Ports of Entry: Aberdeen, Blaine, Point Roberts, Puget Sound (includes Anacortes, Bellingham, Ev- 35
erett, Friday Harbor, Neah Bay, Olympia, Port Angeles, Port Townsend, and Tacoma).

Honolulu District:
Ports of Entry: Hilo, Honolulu, Kahului, Nawili-wili-Port Allen. 40

RAFTING

Boats are rafted when two or more boats secure to one another at anchor. Rafting offers a quick and easy way for boats traveling in a group to spend time together at anchor. Greater weight on limited ground tackle makes rafting an activity that is safe only for predictable and gentle weather conditions.

One boat usually moors with one or two anchors and the others rely on their holding power.

Two boats at the center of the raft might both set anchors in more demanding conditions. Anchors set from more than two boats present a far greater possibility of fouling. If two anchored boats cannot hold, the raft conditions probably are not suitable for rafting.

Rafting boats brings people together similar to opening the fence between two houses except with much less space for the occupants. Raft only with those people you truly want nearby.

The following tips will help make rafting safe and successful.

- **Observe all guidelines for safe anchoring.** Additional scope on a single anchor means more swinging room. Raft well away from obstructions and heavily traveled waterways and channels.

- **Use plenty of docklines and fenders.** Boats rubbing together can quickly run up expensive repair bills. Rig breast lines to keep boats side by side and spring lines to prevent fore and aft movement.

- **Stagger the spreaders.** Align boats so masts and spreaders are not directly opposite each other.

- **Place the largest boat(s) in the middle.** A larger boat, securely anchored, offers greater stability for rafting small boats.

- **Select a position on the raft that fits your departure time.** Tie your boat near the outside of the raft if your plans call for getting underway earlier than others.

Rafted boats make contact somewhere near the beam. Cross the raft at the point where the hulls are closest. Shrouds should be nearby for a secure hand hold. Never try to stabilize boats in a raft by placing hands, arms or legs between boats. When crossing onto the deck at the beam, walk forward of the mast to minimize intrusion on the boat's occupants.

Always respect the wishes of other boaters for privacy and quiet while rafted. The lone boat seeking peace and quiet should anchor away from the raft or leave the raft at sunset as should the lone boat that wants to party through the night.

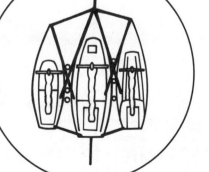

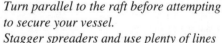

Turn parallel to the raft before attempting to secure your vessel.
Stagger spreaders and use plenty of lines and fenders.

PERMISSION TO BOARD AND COME ALONGSIDE

Much of what we now say and do aboard pleasure boats comes from our nautical heritage. Traditionally, anyone other than crew members wishing to board a ship asks permission of the captain. Unwelcome strangers found aboard might be considered pirates and hung from a yardarm or keel hauled.

Hanging has been replaced by less violent forms of punishment such as dunking, but permission should still be secured before going alongside or stepping aboard another boat. Always respect the rights of a boat at anchor. Any boat approaching with the intention of coming alongside should first ask permission to do so. Never board an unattended, unfamiliar boat unless you are responding to an emergency such as a fire or to re-set the anchor of a dragging boat.

The traditional request "permission to come aboard"and "permission granted" have given way to more familiar phrases. You may choose "O. K. to come aboard" and "sure c'mon aboard", but observe the tradition of seeking permission regardless of your choice of phrase, even when crossing a raft.

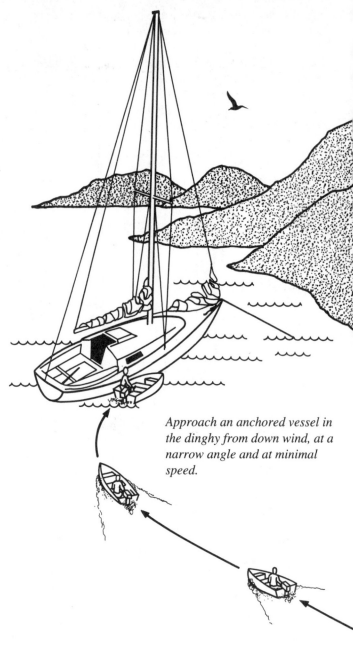

Approach an anchored vessel in the dinghy from down wind, at a narrow angle and at minimal speed.

THE DINGHY

Almost every convenience on a boat hides a corresponding source of aggravation. The dinghy is a good example. Sailors value the ability to shuttle quickly back and forth to shore and to sneak into shallow snorkeling spots. They pay the price for this benefit while maneuvering the sailboat with the dinghy attached or when lifting it and its motor on and off the deck.

Cruising sailors use inflatable (soft) and fiberglass or wood (hard) dinghies. Both can be towed easily behind an auxiliary sailboat with only a slight loss of speed.

Dinghies will capsize when too much weight is concentrated at one point. The stern can usually support more weight than the bow or either side. Teach crew members to step gently into and out of the dinghy. Transfer weight

gradually rather than depositing it suddenly when getting into and out of the dinghy.

Always carry a PFD for each person in the dinghy. Also bring a bailer and the oars despite your motor's reliability. Disconnect the painter from the boat, not the dinghy. You will need it to tie up at your next destination.

Use extreme caution in the dinghy under power. Gather speed slowly and maintain a controllable speed at all times. Travel over waves at a slight diagonal to the bow, something less than 45°. A dinghy can be turned broadside and flipped if a wave crest hits the hull at or near the beam. Practice turning at various speeds and shifting passengers and cargo to get the boat on a plane.

THE OUTBOARD MOTOR

Outboard motors come in a wide variety of shapes and sizes, but they have certain common features.

All outboard motors run on gasoline, but take care to determine whether a motor is two stroke or four stroke. Two stroke motors use fuel that contains a mixture of gasoline and special outboard lubricating oil. Check the manufacturer's instruction book to learn the proper ratio of gas to oil before refueling. Four stroke engines burn plain gasoline and have a lubricating oil reservoir under the engine housing. Find and release the housing latch, lift the housing and check the oil level with its dipstick. Fueling an outboard is critical; putting the wrong type fuel in the tank can cause serious damage to the engine.

Locate the following controls: shift, throttle, choke, starter cord and kill button. Manufacturers sometimes mount a plastic clip on the end of the kill button. A short cord clips onto the boat. The motor automatically stops if the clip is pulled loose. The motor will not start or run if the clip is not installed on the kill button. The gas tank may be built into the top of the motor or it may be a separate container connected to the motor by a hose. Both types have screw-down vents on top of the filler cap. Open by turning counter-clockwise. Somewhere along the hose between the tank and motor locate a large rubber bulb.

Start the outboard by following these steps.

1. **Open the tank vent.**

2. **Pump the bulb (on units without internal tanks) until it becomes hard.**

3. **Shift through the gears and place the gear shift in neutral.**

4. **Ensure that the kill switch is not activated.**

5. **Advance the throttle to start position.**

6. **Pull choke out half-way.**

7. **Place one hand on top of the motor and pull starter cord with the other.**

8. **Always feed the starter cord slowly back into the engine.**

The motor should start after only a few pulls. If not, experiment with the choke and throttle settings. First increase choke. If that fails, push the choke back to 1/2 and add a little throttle. After a total of 8-10 pulls, push the choke in altogether. If the motor fails to start after ten pulls it may require professional help.

A stream of cooling water will flow from somewhere below the engine hood if the cooling system is functioning. Check immediately after starting and stop the motor if no water flows.

Some smaller motors have no gear shift mechanism. Their only options are running slow, running fast or not running at all. Turn the motor entirely around to achieve reverse propulsion.

THE DINGHY AT NIGHT

The dinghy, like the family dog, needs a little attention at bedtime. Repeated contact between an inflatable and a sailboat can rupture or weaken the dinghy's skin. Even though the noise of an inflatable hitting your boat is minimal compared to that created by a hard

dinghy, both types should be secured to avoid hitting the sailboat during the night. Among the options are:

• Secure it with fenders. Use fenders and dock lines to secure the dinghy firmly to either side of the boat.

• Raise it on the transom. Tie the dinghy securely to the transom by pulling it partially onto the sailboat. This works better for inflatables which need fewer fenders.

• Pole it out with the spinnaker or whisker pole. Rig a topping lift and foreguy for the pole and lash it to the shrouds. The dinghy can rest comfortably at the end of the pole without ever hitting the hull.

• Lashing the boom to the shrouds might achieve the same goal as using the pole, but shorter booms may not bring the dinghy far enough outboard to keep it clear of the sailboat.

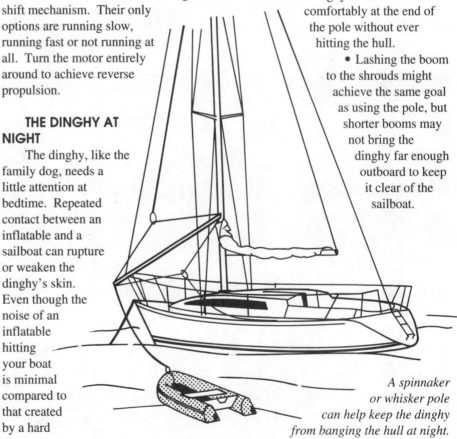

A spinnaker or whisker pole can help keep the dinghy from banging the hull at night.

SWIMMING

Sailboat cruising usually takes place in warm weather and often in places where civilization has not yet fouled water purity. The urge to swim from the boat is as natural as walking barefoot in the sand. The boat, its equipment and the dinghy make perfect platforms for diving, jumping and associated horseplay. Follow a few simple rules and everyone, including those who choose to stay dry (if they can), will enjoy maximum fun at minimum risk.

Never operate the engine with people in the water. Even if you only intend to charge batteries or chill the ice box, the engine should remain off while people swim.

Double check for obstructions. Fixed keel sailboats whose crew correctly prepared for anchoring will be reasonably sure of the absence of underwater obstructions. Anchoring bow and stern allows a boat to come very close to submerged objects with minimum danger of grounding. Alert the crew in such cases.

Check the crew's swimming ability. Make sure everyone's swimming experience matches the prevailing conditions (i. e. current, depth, waves). Have PFDs and other floating objects on deck and in the water.

Elect a lifeguard. Someone onboard should keep swimmers, especially youngsters, in sight from the deck.

Lower the swim ladder. More than one cruising sailboat has disgorged its entire crew immediately after anchoring only to find that no one could climb back aboard over the tall freeboard. This is embarrassing and dangerous.

SECTION IV
REVIEW QUESTIONS

1. A boat anchored by its bow can swing _____ degrees.

2. You must check in with _____ immediately upon entering another country.

3. Boats are _____ when two or more boats secure to one another at anchor.

4. Dinghies will_____ when too much weight is concentrated at one point.

5. Always carry a _____ for each person in the dinghy.

6. _____ stroke engines burn gasoline and have a lubricating oil reservoir under the engine housing.

7. A stream of _____ will flow from somewhere below the engine hood if the outboard is running properly.

8. True or False — Anchoring "bow only" usually requires minimum distance between boats in an anchorage.

9. True or False — Rafted boats make contact somewhere near the beam.

10. True or False — Modern day sailors need no longer ask permission to come alongside and board an unfamiliar boat.

11. True or False — A dinghy can be turned broadside and flipped if a wave crest hits the hull at or near the beam.

12. True or False — Leave the vent on an outboard fuel tank closed during operation.

SAILING SKILLS

Nothing connects a modern cruising sailor with ancient high seas explorers better than arriving at an unfamiliar harbor. We are rarely greeted by semi-naked natives in crude canoes but the thrill of discovery is every bit as real. Safely arriving and securing the vessel calls for skills you have developed prior to and during this course.

PILOTING INTO AN UNFAMILIAR HARBOR

Navigators are tempted to suspend their Dead Reckoning when they make landfall at their new destination. You must continue to use all the available data to find sea buoys or a harbor entrance. Study the chart of the approaching land mass to identify prominent geographical features which become visible. Double check to ensure that the features you see are in fact those on the chart. Also locate charted items such as radio towers and lighthouses. Refer to Coast Pilot and local cruising guides for further descriptions of the safe approach to your intended destination. Written descriptions and diagrams or photos help you apply chart data to the task of getting into the harbor. Take the following steps prior to entering the harbor.

1. **Take a fix as soon as two or three suitable charted items are visible.**

2. **Once you have fixed the boat's location find a position that lines you up for a safe entrance to the harbor. A sea buoy or day beacon is ideal.**

3. **Plot a course to the selected position and adjust the boat's heading, using your hand bearing compass to correct the binnacle compass.**

4. **Fix your position at the selected spot and adjust your course as required to enter the harbor.**

Coastal charts may exclude details inside a harbor. If you do inventory and supplement your chart supply prior to departure you'll have the proper charts. Coast Pilot and cruising guides become invaluable during this part of the journey. Customs, Harbor Patrol, fuel, provisions and other essential information which may not appear on the chart is described in these volumes. You will also find directions to pleasure boat anchorages as well as transient mooring and slip rentals. Locating a group of masts above the water's surface may help orient you when boats, piers, buildings and land obscure your vision. Never hesitate to ask passing boaters for information.

Local law enforcement authorities may be of assistance on channel 16. Hail them by name using normal radio procedure. Use the specific location in your call. For example, Hyannis, Annapolis or Miami. Simply hailing the Harbor Patrol is not sufficient. Your broadcast may reach receivers in several harbors.

You will need to know which agency controls the area. If you hail the Harbor Patrol in an area where the Port Police patrol, you may not get a response. Other boats may be able to give you guidance.

San Juan Channel, the middle one of three principal channels leading from the Strait of Juan de Fuca to the Strait of Georgia, separates San Juan Island
10 from the islands E. It is 13 miles long from its S end to its junction with President Channel at the N end. San Juan Channel is deep throughout and, except near its S entrance, has few off-lying dangers.
Currents.–In the S end of San Juan Channel,
15 between Goose Island and Deadman Island, the average current velocity is 2.6 knots on the flood and ebb, however, maximum flood currents of 5 knots or more cause severe rips and eddies. Daily current predictions for this location may be obtained
20 from the Tidal Current Tables.
Cattle Point, marked by a light and a seasonal fog signal, is the SE extremity of San Juan Island and forms the W point at the S entrance to San Juan Channel. Cattle were once loaded here for shipment
25 to and from Victoria.
Salmon Bank, S of Cattle Point and on the W side of **Middle Channel,** is an extensive shoal covered 1½ to 3 fathoms; it is marked by a lighted gong buoy. Kelp grows on the rocks. **Whale Rocks,** two dark
30 rocks about 5 feet high, are on the E side of Middle Channel 0.6 mile W of Long Island. There are 2¼-fathom spots nearby.

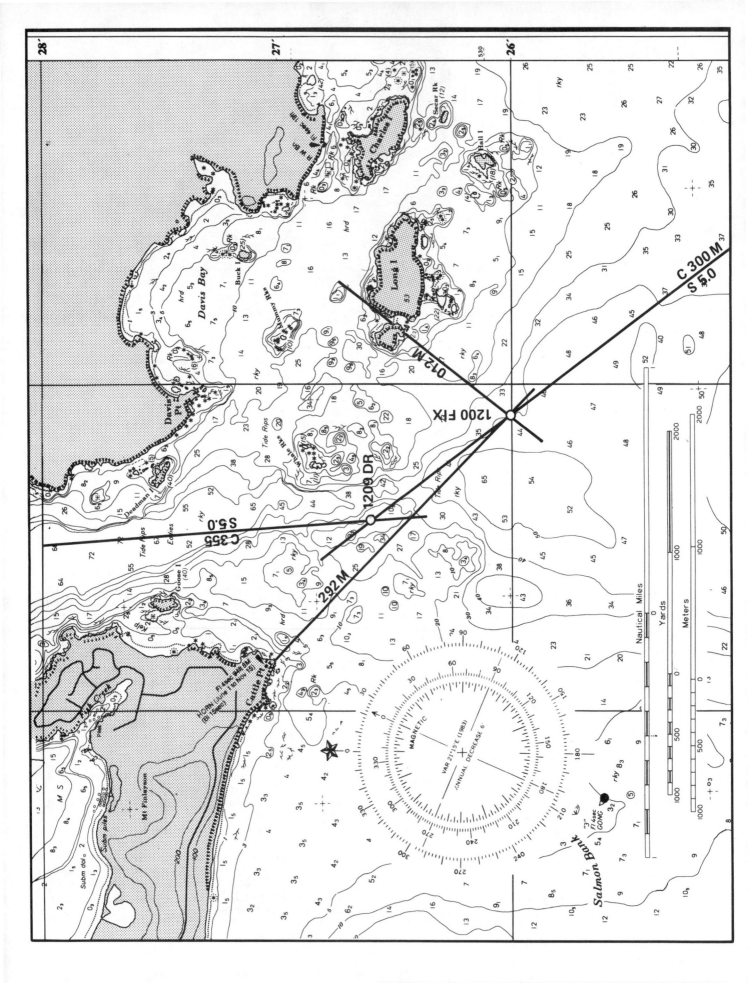

ANCHORING

The qualities to look for in a good anchorage include:

- Shelter from wind, waves and current

- Good holding ground

- Sufficient depth, not too much or too little

- Room to swing with safe scope of anchor rode

Charts supply information on holding ground. Notice the letters "rky" in various places on the sample chart. Chart No. 1 tells you this symbol means a rocky bottom. "S" (sand) "Cl" (clay) or "M" (mud) are all preferable to rock.

Most coastal cruising boats are equipped with one or two varieties of anchor. They match the bottom characteristics of local cruising areas. The Danforth works well on soft bottoms such as sand or mud. Its simple, lightweight design makes it ideal for cruising sailors. A heavier Plow or CQR uses its weight to dig into harder bottoms. Both anchors hold well in areas of moderate bottom hardness. The Plow is more useful in weeds because its weight can cut through and get it on the bottom.

A traditional yachtsman or fisherman anchor is awkward to handle and stow, but it works best on very rocky bottoms where its flukes can wedge themselves between rocks. It may also be useful in matted weeds.

Anchors hold by digging into the bottom. A fifteen pound anchor can hold a 2 ton boat when its flukes bury in the bottom. The anchor becomes lodged in the bottom when the rode tightens.

Scope is the ratio between anchor rode length (from bow to anchor) and distance from anchor cleat or hawse pipe to the bottom. If your bow is 6 feet above the water, the water is 14 feet deep and you have 100 feet of rode out, your scope is 100:20 or 5 to 1. (see diagram)

Greater scope decreases the angle between the rode and the bottom. This means the rode's pull is closer to being parallel to the seabed, allowing the anchor's flukes to point further down, helping it to dig into the bottom. Generally 5 to 1 scope is the minimum for a temporary stay. Use 7 to 1, or greater, for overnight. Chain attached to the anchor helps keep its stock more parallel to the bottom, while resisting chafe damage better than fiber rode.

Use your chart to determine the depth in a selected anchorage. Find the notation in the border of the chart that tells you if Soundings are in Feet, Meters or Fathoms. A fathom, you will remember, is six feet. A meter is 3.1 feet.

Check your depthsounder (if so equipped) to see if the existing conditions match the chart information. Before electronic instruments, sailors measured depth with a lead line. It consisted of a weight (2-5 pounds) and a line. A sailor lowered the weight from the bow and read calibrated depths from the line. He knew the depth when he felt the weight hit the bottom. This method still works in a pinch. Sailors without depthsounders can also ask other boaters in the area what their depthsounders read.

Depths recorded on most NOAA charts reflect mean lower low water. The figures represent the average lowest daily water level. On some days the lowest water level will fall below the charted soundings. You must see a set of tide tables, available where marine books are sold, to determine different depths at high and low tides. The official government publication (see illustration) offers a comprehensive day by day analysis of tides. Other

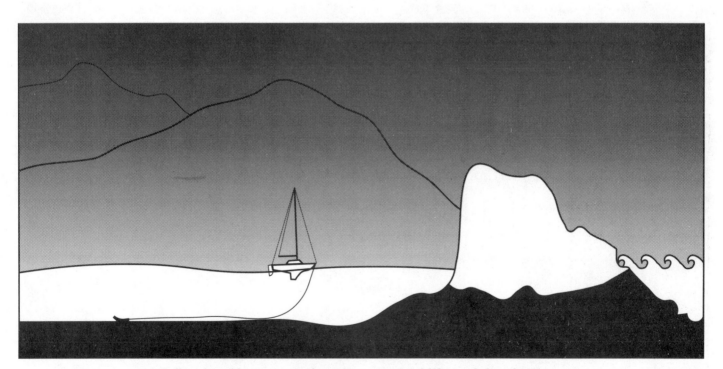

A well anchored boat on a single anchor can swing 360° in a sheltered anchorage.

specialized publications may also give useful data.

To find the time and height of high tide at your location look in the tables for the reference station nearest your intended anchorage; in this case Los Angeles. Times and heights for high and low tides are recorded for each day of the year. Heights preceded by a (-) should be subtracted from the charted depth. Add numbers without the (-).

You may further refine your estimate of water depth if you are anchoring at a subordinate station such as Catalina Harbor. Table 2. indicates that high water is always 11 minutes later and low water is always 17 minutes later than Los Angeles. The height differences of both tides is indicated as a ratio, "*0.94" or 94% of the level at Los Angeles. Table 2. may also indicate height differences preceded by a (+) or (-). These numbers should be added or subtracted rather than multiplied. A combination of both a percentage and a positive or negative height may also be used. For example, "*0.75 +1.3".

Let's suppose you arrive at Catalina Harbor on August 1, about 1200. The chart indicates that the depth is 12 feet in the area where you intend to anchor. In Los Angeles the day's second high tide is expected in an hour and 26 minutes. It will be 4.8 feet above the charted depth. A check of table 2 indicates that high tide comes 11 minutes later and is 94% of the depth at Los Angeles. At high tide, in one hour and 37 minutes, you can expect a total water depth of almost 17 feet.

Low tide comes to Los Angeles at 2027 and to Catalina Harbor at 2044. The depth will be 2.0 feet above the charted depth in L. A. and 94% at Catalina Harbor. Low tide depth is almost 14 feet. Tidal range, the difference between high and low tide, is 2.8 feet.

We have no worries about grounding at anchor in the area we have selected. Anchoring at 1200, nearly high tide, assures us of increased scope at low tide. Anchoring at or near low tide in an area of large tidal range could be more risky. Scope is reduced as the tide rises. A well set anchor could be broken free as the water level rises and the boat's position approaches a spot directly above the anchor. While our example poses no threat of this happening, a wise sailor always takes time to check.

Markings on the anchor rode can make measuring scope a simpler task.

Have the crew remove a sufficient length of rode and flake it on deck. Secure the bitter end if it has not already been tied. Flake the line so it runs off smoothly when the anchor drops. Making flakes about five feet long will allow the crew to count out ten foot lengths every time they pull a layer from the pile. This comes in handy when there are no markings on the rode. Make sure all shackle pins are wired to the shackle. The action created by the boat's movement at anchor can cause the pins to unscrew and set the boat adrift.

Delegate physically capable crew to tend the anchor and rode on deck. Two sets of hands are better than one. Have everyone wear gloves.

TABLE 2. — TIDAL DIFFERENCES AND OTHER CONSTANTS   171

NO.	PLACE	POSITION		DIFFERENCES				RANGES		Mean Tide Level
		Lat.	Long.	Time		Height		Mean Diurnal		
				High water	Low water	High water	Low water			
		° ' N	° ' W	h. m.	h. m.	ft	ft	ft	ft	ft
	Santa Barbara Islands									
457	Wilson Cove, San Clemente Island........	33 00	118 33	-0 03	-0 03	*0.94	*0.94	3.6	5.2	2.7
459	Catalina Harbor, Santa Catalina Island..	33 26	118 30	+0 11	+0 17	*0.94	*0.94	3.6	5.2	2.7
461	Avalon, Santa Catalina Island...........	33 21	118 19	+0 06	+0 09	*0.96	*0.96	3.7	5.3	2.7
463	Santa Barbara Island....................	33 29	119 02	-0 02	+0 04	*0.92	*0.92	3.5	5.1	2.6
465	San Nicolas Island.....................	33 16	119 30	+0 10	+0 21	*0.88	*0.88	3.3	4.9	2.5
467	Prisoners Harbor, Santa Cruz Island.....	34 01	119 41	+0 25	+0 26	*0.90	*0.90	3.4	5.0	2.6
469	Bechers Bay, Santa Rosa Island..........	34 00	120 03	+0 37	+0 35	*0.96	*0.96	3.6	5.3	2.8
471	Cuyler Harbor, San Miguel Island........	34 03	120 21	+0 33	+0 34	*0.94	*0.94	3.5	5.2	2.7

70

LOS ANGELES (Outer Harbor), CALIFORNIA, 1987

Times and Heights of High and Low Waters

	JULY							AUGUST							SEPTEMBER					
Day	Time	Height		Day	Time	Height		Day	Time	Height		Day	Time	Height		Day	Time	Height	
	h m	ft	m		h m	ft	m		h m	ft	m		h m	ft	m		h m	ft	m
1	0634	0.3	0.1	16	0037	4.6	1.4	1	0023	3.7	1.1	16	0353	3.1	0.9	1	1440	5.3	1.6	16	0704	3.9	1.2
W	1336	3.9	1.2	Th	0713	0.5	0.2	Sa	0626	1.6	0.5	Su	0734	2.7	0.8	Tu	2305	0.5	0.2	W	1101	3.4	1.0
	1823	2.9	0.9		1401	5.0	1.5		1326	4.8	1.5		1448	5.1	1.6						1644	4.9	1.5
	2354	4.4	1.3		2023	2.0	0.6		2027	2.0	0.6		2257	0.9	0.3								
2	0706	0.7	0.2	17	0154	3.8	1.2	2	0147	3.1	0.9	17	0623	3.3	1.0	2	0644	3.5	1.1	17	0019	0.4	0.1
Th	1415	4.1	1.2	F	0755	1.2	0.4	Su	0700	2.1	0.6	M	0900	3.1	0.9	W	0927	3.3	1.0	Th	0719	4.1	1.2
	1943	2.7	0.8		1453	5.2	1.6		1416	5.0	1.5		1602	5.2	1.6		1610	5.6	1.7		1156	3.0	0.9
					2157	1.4	0.4		2206	1.4	0.4										1740	5.2	1.6

TIME TO ANCHOR

You have selected an ideal anchoring spot and prepared the crew and ground tackle. The depth and tides have been calculated and you know how much rode to let out for the necessary scope.

1. **Motor slowly upwind to your selected spot.**

2. **Bring the boat to a stop.**

3. **Instruct the crew to ease the anchor out and inform you when it hits the bottom.**

4. **Motor backward.** The crew calls out the amount of rode as it pays out.

5. **At roughly 4 or 5 to 1 scope instruct the crew to tie off or snub the line.** Continue motoring slowly in reverse. A crew member should hold the rode lightly in one hand forward of the cleat. Steady tension on the line will indicate that the anchor is set. Jerking, vibrations or lack of tension indicate that it has not dug in.

6. **Shift to neutral and allow the load to ease from the anchor rode.** The boat may spring forward as the rode tension releases.

7. **Instruct the crew to begin paying out line.**

8. **Motor in reverse until the crew informs you that the proper scope has been reached.** Secure the rode to a cleat.

9. **Repeat step 5.** Bring RPMs up to 1500-2000.

If step 5 fails to set the anchor, follow steps 6 through 9 anyway because the extra scope paid out in step 7 may be enough to make the anchor set. You may find that by the time the anchor digs in, you have moved some distance from the original position. Anchoring may take more than one try. It is always preferable to anchor correctly in daylight with plenty of enthusiastic help, rather than re-anchoring in your underwear, in the middle of the night with a pack of sleep deprived, borderline mutineers.

ANCHOR WATCH

Post a person to serve as an anchor watch for the first few hours after anchoring or anytime when the anchor's holding ability is questionable. This individual takes visual bearings on surrounding landmarks to monitor any change in the boat's position. Sitting in one place in the cockpit the anchor watch can fix objects on land in relation to parts of the boat. Use objects that are not drastically different in their distances from the boat. For example, a certain building may be viewed beside a stanchion at the same time a water tower appears beside a stanchion on the other side of the boat. As the boat swings with the wind the bearing of one object would move forward of its previous position and one would move aft. When the bearings fail to change equally in relation to one another a dragging anchor is probably the cause.

The same result can be achieved with greater precision by using a hand bearing compass. Sight two or three objects and record their bearings. Sighted objects will change bearings equally in relation to one another as a boat swings. For example, the building may bear 030° when the water tower bears 110°. If the boat swung clockwise 25° the building would bear 055° when the water tower bears 135°. You would only conclude the anchor is dragging when the relative increases or decreases are not similar.

An anchor's weight alone will never hold a sailboat in place. This boat will drift uncontrollably from a combination of too little scope and an insufficiently buried anchor.

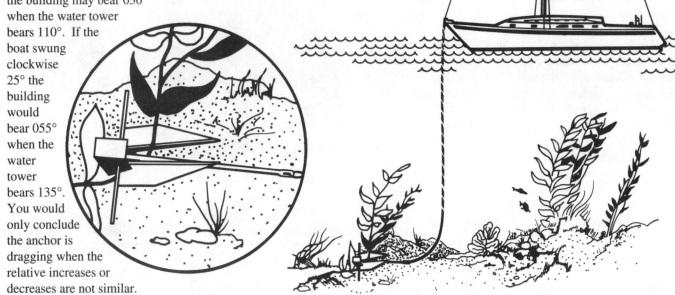

RAISING ANCHOR

The process of retrieving the anchor calls for one person at the helm and one or two on the bow. As the boat moves ahead slowly, the bow crew takes up slack created as the boat approaches the anchor. When the boat gets directly above the anchor further pulling on the rode, the stock draws upward breaking the flukes' hold on the bottom. The anchor then dangles freely at the end of the rode. The helmsman puts the shift in neutral until the anchor has been raised. The bow crew brings anchor, chain and line to the surface by hand or with the aid of a windlass if the boat is so equipped. The rode should be flaked on deck. The helmsman can begin motoring as soon as the bow crew reports that the anchor is clear, and not fouled with lines, power cables or other debris. Motoring forward may force the anchor into the hull while moving in reverse can help clear the anchor.

If the anchor does not break free easily the helmsman can help by motoring past the anchor. Bow crew should tie the rode off to a deck cleat and instruct the helmsman to motor slowly forward. When the anchor breaks free the helmsman shifts back to neutral until the anchor has been raised and is clear.

Anchors often bring up parts of the bottom when they surface. The bow crew should dunk the anchor in and out of the water until mud and weeds have been rinsed away. Bottom mud often has an extraordinary ability to stain decks and crew.

A trip line can be attached to the crown of the anchor allowing you to pull the anchor free from a different direction. Use one in areas where the bottom might be foul with rocks or coral. A simple float such as a fender or bleach bottle marks the trip line at the surface. When the time comes to raise the anchor the boat maneuvers up to the trip line and the crew uses it rather than the rode to dislodge the anchor.

REDUCING SWING

The rights of first arrivals were mentioned in reference to anchoring. Boats anchoring in proximity should make every attempt to swing similarly to avoid a pre-destined invitation to collision. The first boat to anchor dictates the anchoring method used by later arrivals.

BOW AND STERN

The procedures for setting an additional anchor start after being anchored with one anchor from the bow. Set a second anchor off the stern in areas where the wind and/or current remain constant, predictably shift 180° or the wind dies altogether. An area with a daytime sea breeze and nighttime land breeze is a good example. An area with a predictable 90° shift would be a poor choice for bow and stern anchoring. When the wind shifts to the beam, wind resistance on the hull and spars put unnecessary strain on the ground tackle. Wind driven waves from the beam also make the ride at anchor very uncomfortable. Areas with unpredictable, shifty winds would be best suited to another method for reducing swing.

One way to set a stern anchor requires an exceptionally long bow anchor rode. The sailboat must back away from the bow anchor by more than twice the normal scope to create adequate scope for the stern anchor when the boat returns to its

An anchor windlass helps reduce strain on the crew but it may retrieve an anchor slower than two hearty crew members hauling on the rode.

This crew member should use more legs and less back to avoid injury.

Setting the anchor from the dinghy may be preferable for boats with limited bow rode or in shallow areas.

original anchored position. Suppose the depth in the anchorage averages 15 feet and the boat has 5 foot freeboard. We let out 140 feet of bow rode to achieve 7:1 scope. We must have another 140 feet plus an additional 20 to 30 feet in reserve to get far enough away from the bow anchor to properly set a stern anchor.

Prepare for anchoring as you did earlier. Bring the rode on deck in the stern area and secure the bitter end. Flake it on deck so the running end feeds from the top of the coils.

1. **Back away from the bow anchor.** Bow crew pays out line and calls out its length.
   If you intend to use 7 to 1 scope on the stern anchor, back down far enough for 9 or 10 to 1 scope (in our example 180-200 feet). The anchor may not dig in exactly where you drop it. A reduction in scope will result as you pull the anchor forward to set it.

2. **Ease the second anchor to the bottom.**

3. **Motor ahead slowly.** Stern crew pays out anchor rode while bow crew takes up the slack.

4. **Set the second anchor as you did the first.**

5. **Return to your original anchored position.**

   Secure both lines to cleats. Slack the stern anchor rode slightly to allow for rises in the tide.

In an area where the boat cannot safely maneuver to the spot intended for the second anchor or if the first anchor rode cannot be slacked adequately, use the dinghy to do the job. Secure the bitter end of the rode on board. Place someone in the dinghy with the anchor and chain. A second person pays out anchor rode as the dinghy moves away from the boat. The anchor goes overboard when the dinghy has moved far enough away for adequate scope plus an additional distance to allow the anchor some space to dig in. Set the anchor by either winching it toward the sailboat or motoring ahead. Adjust the lines as necessary.

Retrieve the anchor by taking the dinghy back to a position directly above the anchor and pulling it up. A trip line is especially helpful in this instance. It will be more difficult to free an anchor with the dinghy, but pulling it from different directions, using the dinghy's engine, usually does the trick.

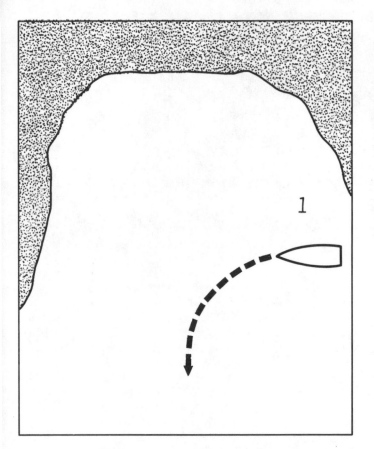

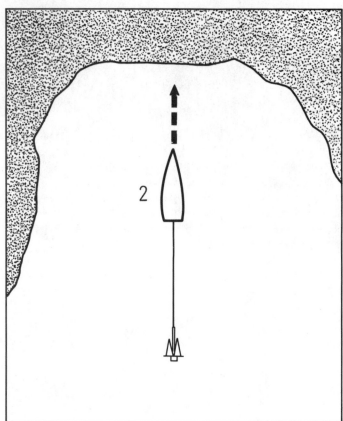

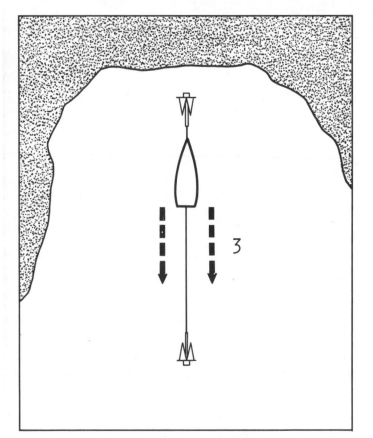

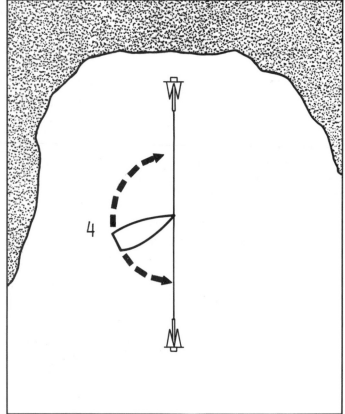

The Bahamian Moor

BAHAMIAN MOOR

Bow and stern anchors keep the boat from moving much except for going up and down with the wind, waves and tide. The boat can be kept in one place with the added benefit of swinging by setting up a Bahamian Moor.

Follow the procedure for anchoring bow and stern. When both anchors are set, lead the stern line to the bow. The boat may now pivot around a single point allowing it to swing in response to shifting winds. Always make sure the anchor rode trails off below the boat at a deep enough angle to avoid fouling by the keel and rudder.

45° OFF THE BOW

Your second anchor will reduce swing if set beside the first anchor so the rodes make an angle of roughly 45°. The boat may travel while suspended between the two anchors but only within a restricted elliptical shaped area. (see diagram) One anchor holds the boat when it moves from the original spot between the two anchors. Both anchors hold the boat once again if conditions push it to a spot at the end of the ellipse, 180° opposite its original position. Two anchors 45° off the bow are a good choice in an area with shifty winds and obstructions nearby. A narrow cove or bay with deep water are examples. Set the first anchor as you would any other anchor off the bow. Remember the boat will set between the anchors and not where it lies with one bow anchor. Bring the second anchor and rode up on deck. Secure the bitter end and flake the rode. Begin motoring. Turn to port or starboard (whichever direction you choose to set the other anchor). Allow the taut anchor rode to keep the boat at the outside of its swinging circle. Avoid jerking the anchor free. When the first anchor rode lies perpendicular to the boat's centerline; with the bow into the wind, drop the second anchor. Back down from the second anchor. Set it as you did the first. Adjust both rodes so the boat sits with equal scope and strain on both anchors.

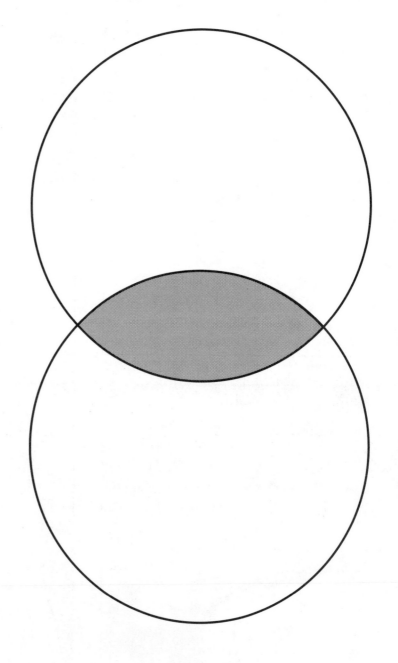

A boat anchored with two anchors approximately 45° off the bow has one swinging circle for each anchor. The shaded area indicates where the boat can swing when the two circles are combined.

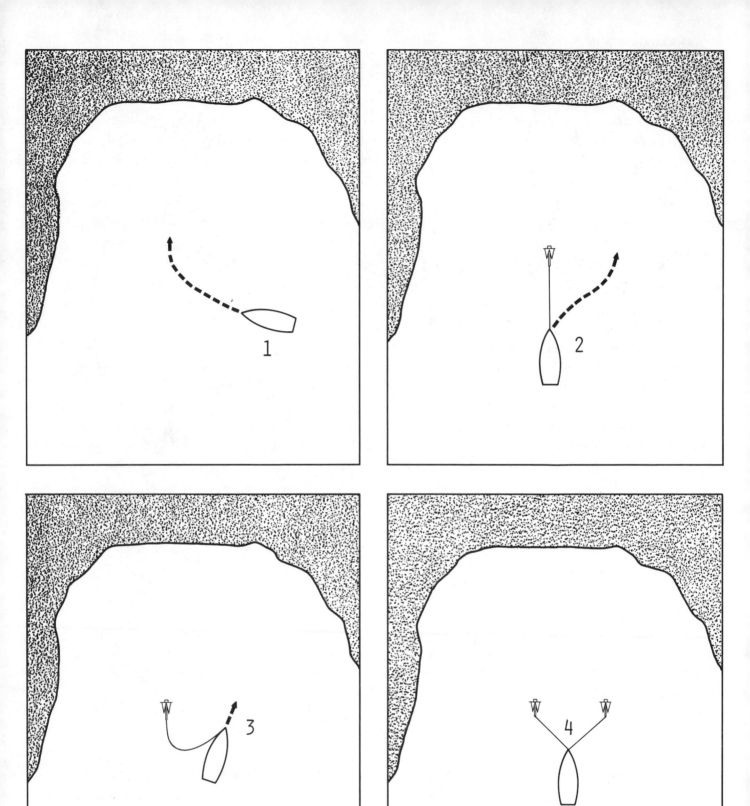

Setting two anchors at 45° off the bow.

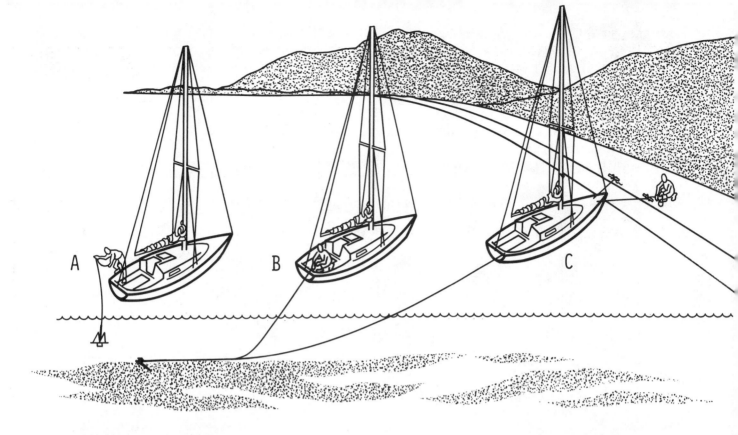

MEDITERRANEAN MOORING

The choicest locations for mooring in many Mediterranean harbors lie along a seawall called the quay. No finger piers jut out from the quay so sailors use an anchor to control either the bow or stern, while the other end attaches directly to the quay. This method of securing has become known as a Mediterranean Moor and sailors traveling in that part of the world have opportunities to develop the necessary skills in all kinds of challenging conditions.

Skipper and crew must decide which end of the boat to attach to the quay. Strong cross winds or currents make setting the stern hook preferable to an anchor off the bow. The boat maneuvers more effectively in forward than in reverse. While the boarding ladder and open stern pulpit make fastening the stern better suited for loading people and equipment, you may not want the town's population peering into your cockpit and cabin. Make your plan well in advance and execute it confidently.

Follow your tried and true anchoring procedure. Achieving correct scope can be tricky. The boat can only travel a set distance from the anchor before running into the quay. Try estimating distance in boat lengths. You know how far 35' or 40' is because you can see the length of the deck. You should be able to calculate additional boat lengths with reasonable accuracy. Set the anchor well, guard against strong onshore winds. Also set the anchor slightly upwind or up current of other lines.

Have plenty of fenders handy to avoid contact with the quay and adjacent boats. Crossing and lengthening stern docklines reduces strain in areas of severe tidal range. Avoid crossing neighbors' anchor rodes.

BREAST LINE

A strong surge or wind driven waves can cause your hull to pound against a dock or seawall while tied alongside. Place an anchor to windward and use it to hold off and avoid damage. Follow the same procedure for a Mediterranean Moor except lead the line to a midships cleat or winch and tension the rode as conditions dictate. Anchoring may be restricted in some harbors. Maintain an anchor watch on deck to keep menacing propellers away.

PICKING UP A MOORING

Many harbors have permanent moorings available for use by transients. The mooring usually consists of an anchor, a chain or heavy line connecting the anchor to the buoy, a ball shaped buoy, and a mooring pendant. The pendant may have an additional small float to make it easier to retrieve from the deck of a boat. Otherwise, it attaches to the top of the mooring ball and rests in the water. The bow crew catches the pendant with a boat hook. It usually ends in an eye that will fit over the boat's bow cleat. The mooring line can be very short because the mooring's heavy, buried anchor makes scope less critical. Moorings are usually preferable to anchoring because more boats can fit safely and comfortably in a smaller area. Unlike your anchor and rode, an unfamiliar mooring's condition cannot be easily inspected. Use caution in such circumstances.

Use the following method to pick up a mooring:

1. **Approach slowly on an upwind heading.**

2. **Position a crew member on the bow.** That individual relays directions via hand signals (see diagram) to the helmsman once the mooring gets too close to the bow for the helmsman to see.

3. **Glide the final few feet in neutral on directions from the bow crew.**

4. **The bow crew retrieves the mooring pendant and attaches it to the deck cleat.**

5. **The boat eases to leeward of the mooring.**

Some moorings have a second anchor and pendant for the stern. A connecting line runs between the bow and stern pendants. Once the bow mooring is secure locate the connecting line and follow it hand over hand while walking to the stern of the boat. The stern pendant should surface after some pulling. An anchor watch is not necessary as long as the pendants have been firmly attached to deck cleats.

CASTING OFF A MOORING

Leaving the mooring is the reverse of picking it up. If bow and stern pendants are attached, cast the leeward pendant off first. Assuming the wind did not shift 180°, you are left moored by the bow pendant. Motor ahead slowly. The bow crew will call out when the line is slack. The helmsman shifts to neutral and pendant, float and connecting line all go overboard.

Allow the wind to help in these operations as long as the maneuver poses no threat of collision. Motoring quickly toward the mooring ball increases the risk of catching the hawser or connecting line in the prop. Often the wind turns the boat and pushes it clear of the mooring and adjacent boats. Otherwise, wait a few seconds for the lines to sink and then get steerage way on. Select the least obstructed course out of the mooring area and head for open water.

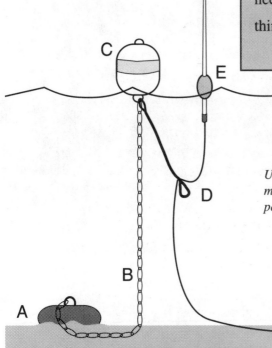

Underwater view of a typical mooring. (A) anchor, (B) chain, (C) buoy, (D) mooring pendant, (E) float and wand, (F) connecting line, (G) stern pendant, (H) stern anchor

SECTION V

PROBLEM SOLVING & TROUBLE SHOOTING

"At this instant, while Gaggoo, on the summit of the head, was clearing the whip - which had somehow got foul of the great cutting tackles - a sharp, cracking noise was heard; and to the unspeakable horror of all, one of the two enormous hooks suspending the head tore out, and with a vast vibration the enormous mass sideways swung, till the drunk ship reeled and shook as if smitten by an iceberg."

Moby Dick
— Herman Melville

Murphy's proverbial law, "Everything that can go wrong will go wrong", has convinced some hapless sailors that Murphy must have been a fellow mariner. Apply more logic and a sounder analysis emerges. A boat contains a plethora of mechanical and electrical equipment and systems. It travels in an often unpredictable environment . An important part of your sailing education focuses on identifying potential problems and taking precautions to minimize their risk. You check the oil, pump the bilge and perform a radio check to eliminate these variables from the list of potential problems.

Unfortunately, even the most thorough preparation cannot totally eliminate the chance of mishaps. Mechanical failures and other unexpected events require you to quickly and accurately assess the situation, then execute the most effective solution within your means. As always, safety of the crew and vessel take highest priority.

Section V explores some of the problems most likely to face an intermediate level cruising sailor and discusses the best ways to cope with them when they occur.

DRAGGING ANCHOR

Your carefully anchored boat could move from its intended anchorage for a number of reasons. Dragging anchor or pulling the anchor free of its hold on the bottom occurs more frequently than many boaters would like to admit. Most of the causes have been addressed previously. They include inadequate scope, increased wind, an incorrect choice of anchor for the holding ground and interference from other boats and their anchors.

If prevention was ineffective a cure must be implemented. Determine if your new position poses any danger from obstructions or other boats or if the anchor is still dragging. If so, you need to re-anchor. Follow the procedures for raising the anchor and re-anchoring. Try to ascertain why your anchor dragged. If necessary, change anchors, use more scope or select a spot with better holding ground.

If you have enough sea room to avoid re-anchoring try simply increasing scope by letting out more rode. Even a poor choice of anchor for the holding ground can sometimes be overcome by increasing scope. Start the engine and back down against the anchor after letting out more rode. Station a bow crew to feel the anchor line as you did in Section IV. Post an anchor watch after re-anchoring or increasing scope.

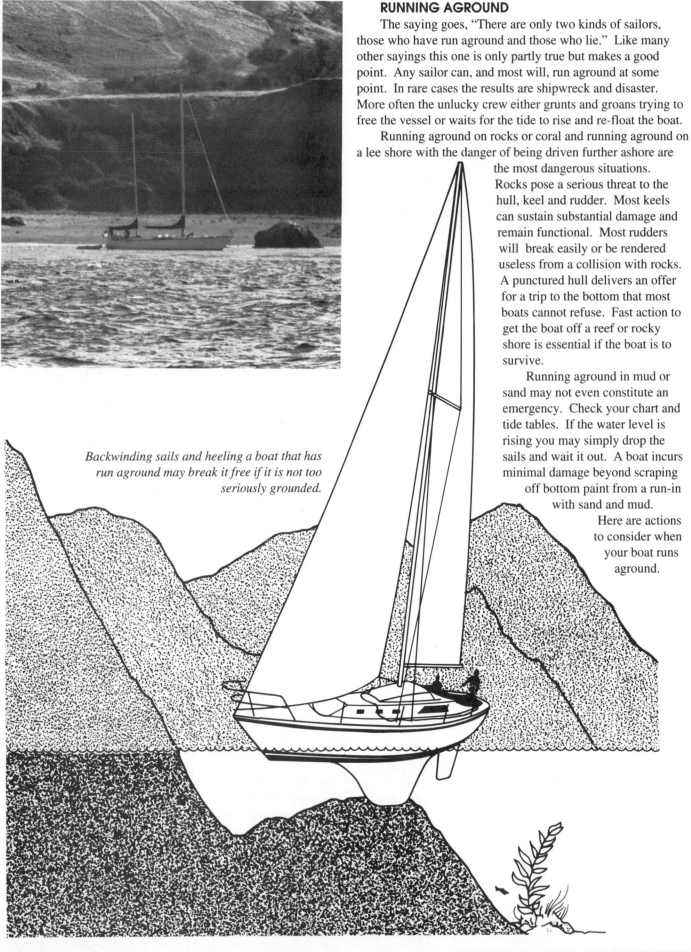

RUNNING AGROUND

The saying goes, "There are only two kinds of sailors, those who have run aground and those who lie." Like many other sayings this one is only partly true but makes a good point. Any sailor can, and most will, run aground at some point. In rare cases the results are shipwreck and disaster. More often the unlucky crew either grunts and groans trying to free the vessel or waits for the tide to rise and re-float the boat.

Running aground on rocks or coral and running aground on a lee shore with the danger of being driven further ashore are the most dangerous situations. Rocks pose a serious threat to the hull, keel and rudder. Most keels can sustain substantial damage and remain functional. Most rudders will break easily or be rendered useless from a collision with rocks. A punctured hull delivers an offer for a trip to the bottom that most boats cannot refuse. Fast action to get the boat off a reef or rocky shore is essential if the boat is to survive.

Running aground in mud or sand may not even constitute an emergency. Check your chart and tide tables. If the water level is rising you may simply drop the sails and wait it out. A boat incurs minimal damage beyond scraping off bottom paint from a run-in with sand and mud.

Here are actions to consider when your boat runs aground.

Backwinding sails and heeling a boat that has run aground may break it free if it is not too seriously grounded.

Ease the sheets. Avoid forcing the boat further aground by spilling power from the sails.

Jibe immediately. While running or reaching, a quick jibe could heel the boat enough in the right direction to keep it from becoming completely stuck. Do so only if deeper water can be found on the other jibe.

Motor in reverse. You were in deeper water moments before the brakes locked. Lowering the sails and powering the engine in reverse might get you back there. Watch the temperature gauge. Debris from the bottom can clog the raw water strainer and cause the engine to overheat.

Shift weight. Shifting all movable ballast to the bow or to one side, plus a kick from the propeller with the rudder over, could create enough leverage to free the keel.

Heel using the boom. Lash the boom to the shrouds on the side with deeper water and shift as much weight and movable ballast (people) out on the boom as is safe. A halyard rigged to the outboard end of the boom will support the weight.

Kedge off with an anchor . Use the dinghy or another boat to set an anchor in deeper water. Then winch, windlass or pull the boat free. Attach a halyard to the kedge. Winching on a halyard will cause the boat to heel and possibly free the keel while drawing the boat toward deeper water. Set the kedge in excess of one masthead length from the boat to ensure effectiveness.

Accept a tow. A fellow boater may tow you into deep water. Always determine whether the other boat intends to tow you out of kindness or a profit motive before you accept a towing hawser. Fasten the towing hawser to a strong cleat or winch and observe applicable safety precautions.

Avoid staying in an area that completely dries at low tide. Most modern sailboats have not been designed to support the hull's weight on one small point. Structural damage could occur, especially if the rising or falling tide brings waves that bounce the hull on the bottom. Check the chart and daily tide tables to predict the future changes in water level.

If the circumstances leave no choice but to wait for the tide to drop farther before it rises enough to refloat you, position the boat so it tips with the mast pointing toward the shallow water side. Water is less likely to flood the cabin when the boat rests with the keel pointing offshore. Seal the cabin. Place all available fenders and cushions under the hull as it begins to settle on the ground.

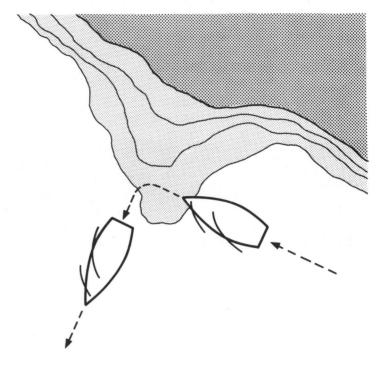

A quick jibe after running aground on a broad reach or run might free the keel. This solution assumes there is enough maneuverability to jibe and there is deeper water in the new direction.

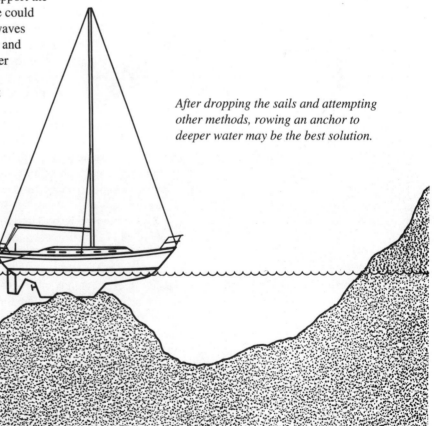

After dropping the sails and attempting other methods, rowing an anchor to deeper water may be the best solution.

ENGINE FAILURE WHILE UNDERWAY

A later portion of Section V examines some causes and solutions for engine failure. You must be prepared to deal with a sudden loss of power while underway. If immediate re-starting of the engine proves impossible quick thinking can avoid collision.

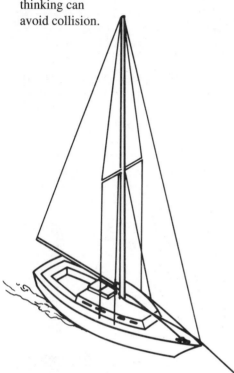

IN AN ANCHORAGE

The skipper's decision making skill comes into play in this situation. A sudden engine failure usually occurs while the boat is moving through the anchorage. The skipper may still be able to follow his original course without power unless he was preparing to back down and slow the boat to avoid a nearby obstruction. In such cases immediately steer for clear, deep, open water.

Next the skipper must decide what poses the most immediate danger. Will the boat glide to a stop and begin drifting into other boats or shallow water? If other boats pose an immediate threat, assign crew members to fend off and man fenders. Rig dock lines for rafting to another boat if the opportunity presents itself.

Successful anchoring can take the immediacy and danger out of the situation. Unless the crew had been preparing to anchor, you can expect a slow response from all but the most professional crews.

Knowing this the skipper must realize that part-way through anchoring he may need to divert some hands to fending-off. Anchoring may not be a realistic alternative if the boat cannot reach a suitable spot. You may not have sufficient momentum to reach a windward location, so look for a leeward anchorage.

Sailing out may be possible with plenty of wind and clear water. If conditions are right, start sailing at your earliest opportunity. It may not be possible after attempting other solutions. Bigger, heavier boats take more time and power to get moving. Always keep halyards attached to their sails and jib sheets ready on the primary winches until the boat has been anchored or docked. A roller furling genoa can usually roll into service quicker than a mainsail.

IN A CHANNEL

In most channels, especially those serving commercial vessels, regulations restrict anchoring. An anchored vessel presents a hazard to less maneuverable vessels which cannot leave the channel. Always try to guide the boat out of traffic before anchoring. If you see a strong possibility of collision with another vessel or obstruction save the boat by the available means, including anchoring. Use VHF radio or any other means available to let approaching boats or ships know you are unable to maneuver. You may end up dealing with local law enforcement authorities but that inconvenience pales when compared to putting your boat on the rocks.

If shallow water lines the channel's edges you can intentionally run aground. Although we normally try to avoid this, on a soft bottom it may be preferable to drifting in a heavily travelled channel. Law enforcement authorities, especially the Coast Guard, have adopted more restrictive towing policies in recent years. Your situation must be thoroughly menacing before they offer a tow. Most U. S. waterways have commercial towing service available. They monitor channel 16 and respond promptly to requests for help. Temporarily running aground can provide time to radio for a tow. Signaling passing boaters may also yield assistance.

If the outboard is still mounted on the dinghy, the dinghy can let you regain control of a boat whose engine has failed. Rig the dinghy to tow with a bow line, push from astern, or made up tightly on either quarter.

Gentle persuasion may help unwrap a line from the propeller, but don't count on it.

LINES AROUND THE PROPELLER

Despite your efforts to ensure that all lines are aboard before engaging the propeller, occasionally a line finds its way into the water and wraps itself around the prop. It usually happens during periods of heightened activity and further complicates a trying situation. Try these simple solutions before resorting to more extreme methods.

Pull on the line. Turn the engine off and place the shift in neutral. Pull the line back onto the boat by hand. Never use a winch. Excess force could bend the shaft or pull the strut loose. If it's just a minor wrap you may have favorable results.

Reverse the prop. First try turning the propeller shaft backward by hand. Send someone below to the transmission and locate the circular metal coupling that attaches the propeller shaft to the aft part of the transmission. It should be big enough to get your hands around and turn. You must know whether the boat

has a left or right hand propeller in order to rotate the shaft in the correct direction.

Reversing the propeller using the engine may also work, but it entails a certain risk. A badly tangled line can become further tangled and exert pressure on the propeller, shaft and strut. Try this only as a last resort before sending someone overboard.

Start the engine. Idle it down to minimum RPMs. Free the topside end of the line if it has been pulled taut by the propeller. Shift quickly in and out of reverse while someone with gloves pulls the line if it begins to untangle. Do not repeat this tactic unless it produces the desired results.

Send someone overboard. A patient person with the free end of the line and a marlin spike may be able to keep the line in one piece. You can reasonably expect that the line will emerge shorter and less tenacious after its meeting with the propeller.

EMERGENCY TILLER

In section II you located the rudder post and its extension. You also discovered that the steering mechanism may occasionally break down. The emergency tiller fits onto the rudder post extension to give you rudder control when the normal system fails. Always locate the emergency tiller and assemble it during your familiarization tour on the boat. Make sure you understand how its pieces fit together and what, if any, parts of the boat must be disassembled to make it work. You may need to remove a cover plate or the steering wheel. Know what tools you will need for each task and where they are stored.

The mechanism connecting the wheel to the rudder may jam or seize and make it impossible to move the rudder with the emergency tiller. The solution is to disassemble the cables, chain or hydraulic arm. The procedure and tools should be worked out in advance. Practice steering the boat using the emergency tiller. Emergencies usually come as a surprise, remedies should never be surprising.

Emergency tillers will facilitate steering but usually place the helmsman in some awkward position.

LEAKS AND FLOODS

Boats stay afloat by creating a cavity of buoyant air that rests happily on the water's surface. Sailboats made of cement and huge steel ships float as long as their hulls separate the air inside from the water outside. Replace the air with water and the boat sinks like cement, steel or fiberglass is intended to sink.

Water can enter the hull from a variety of sources. Any unrestricted opening below the water line can sink the boat. Monitor water level in the bilge at least daily. Normally it varies only slightly unless the boat springs a leak. People usually fail to notice leaks until they step into the cabin and swamp their shoes.

Water in the cabin does not always indicate flooding. Sinks, heads and open hatches can admit a generous amount of water without causing a threat of sinking. It may take a few minutes but the flow of water should subside after securing one of these. If not, continue your investigation.

Bilge water can come from three sources; the water around you, a ruptured fresh water tank, or the holding tank. Fresh water or holding tanks flowing into the bilge cause concern but not alarm. Eliminate some possibilities with a few simple tests. Smell the bilge; your nose will tell you if the holding tank has begun spilling its contents. When cruising in salt water, once the holding tank has been eliminated as a source, you may try tasting the water. No salt taste means the water is not coming from outside the hull.

The following steps should be followed immediately upon discovering rising water levels in the bilge.

1. **Activate bilge pumps.** Switch on all electric pumps that have not activated automatically. Assign crew to manual pumps. Select a reserve person to provide others with rest, without a pump interruption.

2. **Get non-essential crew on deck.** Put on PFD's.

3. **Locate the source of the leak.** Make an orderly check of all potential points of water entry. Close through-hulls as you go to gain added peace of mind.

4. **Stop the leak.** Use soft wood plugs in through-hulls and other rounded holes. Temporary hull patching material available from marine stores might help with odd shaped and larger holes. Rags stuffed into holes with tools or other objects can also stop or slow a leak. Stop leaking or ruptured pipes by wrapping them with tape or plastic wrapping, covered by tightly bound canvass and many turns of strong cord.

Watch the water level when the bilge pumps start operating at maximum capacity. If the water level drops you have time to gain control of the situation. If it continues rising your options are limited.

You want, most of all, to find and stop the leak; but if the water rises so far it swamps the batteries and shorts out electrical circuits, the engine and electrical system will quit. Assign a competent crew member to stand-by the radio, ready to call other boats or send out a May Day before you lose power. In very severe cases, start making preparations to abandon ship.

The cases of losing a boat operated by competent, well trained people are indeed rare, but *Cruising Fundamentals* would be negligent in its duty if the subject was not addressed.

FIRE FIGHTING

Fire extinguishers are not optional when boats carry built-in fuel tanks. There are three main types of fire: Class A fires involve combustible material that leaves an ash (wood, fabric); Class B fires are flammable liquids (oil, alcohol); Class C fires are electrical. Extinguishing agents may be effective against one, two or all three types and the extinguisher container will reflect this. Coast Guard regulations require you to carry Type B extinguishers (see Section II for number and size) but combination (AB, BC, or ABC) units will satisfy the rule, provided they are Coast Guard approved. (need photo of fire extinguisher)

Most extinguishers operate by removing a safety pin or clip and squeezing a handle grip at the top of the extinguisher. Aim the extinguishing agent at the base of the fire and use a sweeping motion to kill it. Discharge in short bursts. Immediate action with an extinguisher on a small fire will keep it from growing. Speediness usually spells the difference between success and failure because most extinguishers will exhaust their charge in less than 30 seconds.

Fight a Class A fire with water or a combination extinguisher; make sure there are no lingering embers. Fight Class B fires with CO_2 (in enclosed spaces) or dry chemical agents. Secure the electrical power in a Class C fire; then handle it as a Class A fire.

Knowing the type of extinguishing agents you have and their characteristics can save you a lot of grief. Dry chemicals are extremely effective but very messy; clean-up will take forever and they have a fatally corrosive effect on electronics. CO_2 is good in an unoccupied, enclosed space. Halon is very effective below and also clean; great for galley fires but not too good topside where the wind will blow the agent away.

Know what kind of extinguishers you have, where they are and how they operate. Inspect them periodically to be sure they are ready for use.

TROUBLE SHOOTING

Many sailors treat the engine like an angry watchdog. Leave it in its cage, feed it occasionally and ignore it as long as it does its job. Occasionally the engine, like the dog, fails to bark upon command. Unlike the dog, the diesel engine generally returns to its reliable self after a few simple adjustments. A basic understanding of what might ail your marine diesel will help bring man and beast into closer harmony.

ENGINE COOLING FAILURE

Your understanding of the cooling system makes the job of problem solving much easier. A cooling system failure usually means the closed system stopped circulating or the raw water system stopped circulating. Either problem causes the engine temperature to rise and, if left unrepaired, the closed system will overheat. The closed system behaves the same as a car radiator when it overheats. Steam and fluid escape from the filler cap.

On a boat the cabin fills with gaseous coolant creating a petro-chemical environment which is not conducive to life as we know it. This is reason enough to make a habit of checking the engine gauges and the water flowing out with the exhaust. Turn the engine off immediately if water fails to flow or steam escapes from the closed system.

CLOSED SYSTEM FAILURE

If the engine overheats but the raw water discharge flows normally with the exhaust, then the closed system has a problem. The following are potential solutions.

Fluid Level: It could be as simple to fix as adding water to the coolant reservoir, but don't count on it. If the level is low, there is probably a leak. Do not open the filler until the engine has had time to cool. The expansion tank under the filler should no longer be hot to the touch. Replace the fluid, start the engine and fill any additional space created by trapped air escaping. Replace the cap.

There is a slight possibility that the aggregate effect of small overflows during hot running periods could cause a serious drop in fluid level. This will not occur if fluid levels are checked regularly. If the problem was a gradual depletion of fluid; after refilling, the temperature should go up to the 180-200 degree range and stay there after the engine runs for 15 to 20 minutes.

Leaking Hoses: Low fluid level usually occurs because of a leak. Replace the fluid and cap the expansion tank. Start the engine. Trace the hoses and lines that make up the closed system. As the water in the system heats up, pressure will force fluid out through any crack or hole.

Without spare parts your only option is to run the engine sparingly. Leave the filler cap loose. The engine will overheat eventually but the lack of pressure should buy some extra motoring time.

Thermostat: A hot engine block makes the atomized diesel fuel ignite thoroughly and efficiently. The thermostat ensures that the block reaches an acceptable temperature quickly by closing off part of the water circulation path and trapping hot water in the block. Only after the temperature has reached the prescribed level will the thermostat open and allow water to circulate throughout the system. A broken or stuck thermostat fails to open and causes the engine to overheat.

Check the owner's manual to be sure your boat is equipped with a thermostat. If so, it will be under a cast flange or housing bolted to the engine block. A large diameter hose attaches to it. Remove the thermostat by removing nuts holding the housing to the block. Be careful not to damage the paper gasket between the housing and the block. The thermostat sits underneath the housing and will pop out with a little prying from a screwdriver. Replace the housing. Avoid overtightening the nuts.

Follow the directions above for replacing lost coolant. If the thermostat caused the overheating the problem will be solved once it has been removed. This is an emergency procedure; replace the thermostat as soon as possible to avoid further complications.

Coolant filler cap is found somewhere high on the engine.

Belt Tension: One of the engine's belts drives the water pump. Check for a broken or loose belt.

The key to tensioning a belt lies in finding the adjustment. Most belts run over two or three pulleys. A fairly typical set-up includes one for the engine, one for the water pump and one for the alternator. The engine and water pump pulleys are stationary. The alternator's position is adjustable. The alternator is attached with bolts and/or nuts in two or three places. One of these fasteners connects to an arm with a slot in it. This is the adjustment. Follow the steps below to adjust tension on a belt with an adjustable alternator.

1. **Loosen the adjusting bolt or nut and any other bolts that hold the alternator.**

2. **Make sure the belt runs smoothly over all pulleys.**

3. **Pry the alternator housing away from the engine with a very long screwdriver or a pry bar.** Use leverage against the metal alternator housing. Do not pry against anything other than solid metal parts.

4. **Tighten the adjusting bolt.** Hold the pry bar to sustain belt tension with one hand and tighten the adjusting bolt on its bracket with the other.

5. **Tighten the other nuts and bolts.** If the belt needing attention does not drive an alternator, another component in the loop will have the adjustment. Adapt the procedure to the situation.

The adjusting bolt, to the left of the bolt being tightened, was tightened first.

RAW WATER SYSTEM FAILURE

If there was little or no raw water cooling discharge with the exhaust, begin your investigation with that system. You are already familiar with the system's components so tracing a failure should be easy. Start by looking for broken or disconnected hoses.

THE STRAINER

Next look for blockage in the strainer. Look through the bowl at the screen. If debris is present it should be visible. Clear the screen using the following procedure.

1. **Close the intake through-hull.**

2. **Remove the bowl or metal cover.** The bowl may be attached in a number of ways. Generally, it is easily removed with a wrench or pair of pliers. Some may have threads cut into the rim of the bowl. This type will screw into the metal bracket and seat with a rubber gasket.

3. **Clean the screen.** Small particles can be flushed out by running water through the middle of the screen and lightly brushing the outer surface. Larger material can be removed by hand.

4. **Replace the screen and bowl or metal cover.** Make sure the gasket is in place and the bowl is properly seated.

5. **Open through-hull.**

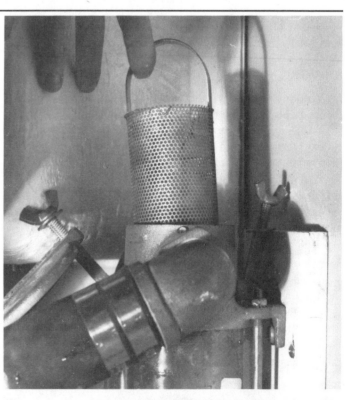

Objects may become lodged in the through-hull valve. Before anything else, try opening and closing the valve repeatedly. You may be able to separate the portion outside the hull from the debris in the line. The part inside will end up in the strainer unless it is too big to pass through the hose. Follow the instructions below in such cases.

Sadly, our waterways have become littered with plastic film from bags, wrappings and other sources. It never decomposes. It floats and it occasionally finds its way into through-hulls that bring cooling water to the engine.

You may be able to see part of a bag or other debris by closing the through-hull and removing the attached hose. Loosen the hose clamp with a screwdriver and free the hose from the fitting with a twisting motion.

An obstruction may be lodged in the fitting and not be visible from the engine compartment. If nothing is visible and you wish to confirm that no obstruction exists beyond your view, open the through-hull. A fountain of water will pour into the boat if the passage is clear. Slip a length of hose over the fitting and divert the flow away from anything electrical, such as the starter motor, mounted near the through-hull.

Unfortunately, if you can see part of the debris, some of it will be stuck in the through-hull. Sometimes you can clear a path by opening the valve and pulling the plastic through. Be prepared for the flood of water that will also come through. If the volume of material beyond the valve is too great to pull through, put the hose back together, disconnect the other end of the hose, open the sea valve and blow through the hose to clear the debris. If that fails, send someone overboard to pull it free.

IMPELLER

Once you know the intake line is not broken or obstructed the only other serviceable item in the raw water system is the impeller. As you discovered earlier, the impeller housing attaches to the engine with a hose coming in and one going out. The impeller itself has a set of rubber fin-like vanes and turns on a shaft inside the housing. Eventually the rubber vanes wear out and break off causing water to stop flowing. Replacing the impeller at sea is feasible if you have another one onboard. There may be some short term benefit to removing broken vanes from inside the housing even without replacing the impeller. This may allow the few remaining vanes to pump some water. Remove the impeller by following these steps.

1. **Close the through-hull fitting.**

2. **Remove the impeller housing face plate.** It attaches with screws or small hex bolts. Be careful not to loosen the fasteners or damage the paper gasket which seals the plate to the cast housing.

3. **Pry the impeller off its shaft.** Remove the impeller by positioning the tips of two flathead screwdrivers under the impeller and gently prying against the rim of the housing. You may also grasp the impeller hub with pliers and pull it straight off. If there is a snap ring in a groove at the end of the shaft use snap ring pliers or careful coaxing with a screwdriver to pry the ring free.

4. **Replace the impeller and snap ring.**

5. **Replace the faceplate.** Tighten the screws/bolts in two steps. First tighten them until they just touch the plate. Then snug them a fraction of a turn until they are well seated. Be careful not to use more force than the bolt's thin shaft can withstand. Also, rather than beginning with one and going around in a circle, follow an alternating sequence which brings you diagonally across the plate each time.

If overheating persists after checking all of the serviceable items mentioned above, it probably needs a mechanic. Broken

A new impellor with its fins intact

water pumps and blockage in the cooling system are not easily repaired while on passage.

You can reach your destination even if overheating persists after the solutions above have been exhausted. Sailors are fortunate because they can make progress as long as the wind blows. Remember that a cold engine will run for ten to twenty minutes before completely overheating. Plan your voyage accordingly. Sail as long as possible and save the engine for use at the last minute. Coordinate the crew so that when the engine starts, the boat immediately makes progress to its destination. Have the anchor and rode ready to go if anchoring is planned. Lowering and folding or furling sails can be done on the way to or at the anchorage or dock.

Pilots know how long their aircraft will stay aloft after losing power; and when the engines quit they look for an appropriate place to land. Sailors with an overheating engine have the same window of opportunity from the time they turn the engine on until it overheats. Plan your landing accordingly.

ENGINE FAILURE

The sun rises in the east, water flows downhill and anything mechanical can break. We take a little liberty by adding the last statement to the laws of nature, but not much. Mechanical failures are usually unexpected but they should never come as a shock. Everything that spins, grinds or pumps is made up of pieces. When one or more pieces fails to do its job, the entire machine quits. In the case of an inboard diesel engine, simple solutions can make the difference between a temporary inconvenience and total debility.

ELECTRICAL SYSTEM

Everyone recognizes the sounds a car makes when it starts. The whining that comes from turning the key is the starter motor. It runs on electrical power from the car's battery. Once the car starts it runs because electrical current from the battery feeds power to the spark plugs. Turn the key off and the power flow stops and so does the engine.

If you hear the starter while activating the key and/or starter button, move on to ENGINE PROBLEMS. The following information applies if you hear a click or no sound at all. Start searching for problems at the most accessible part of the system; in this case the battery switch. The switch channels current from either of two batteries to the house electrical system. It also links the two batteries for more power. If one battery dies completely the combination, on the "All" or "Both" setting, will be weakened because the dead battery drains power from the charged one. Switch to one battery, then the other and attempt to start the engine again. Check the system voltage. Any reading below 12 indicates a battery charge low enough to prevent the starter from turning fast enough to start the engine. If both batteries appear discharged proceed to jump the batteries.

JUMPING THE BATTERIES

In some cases the battery switch is accessible from the back. Locate the cables leading to and from the switch. Check each one and make sure it is tightened down snugly onto the switch. A loose cable could be the problem. If access to the back of the switch requires unscrewing panels, leave the switch in favor of more accessible components. Search for the back of the switch later if your remaining investigation proves fruitless.

If battery switching fails to bring the starter to life open the battery compartment. Take the covers off the battery boxes. Remove the caps on top of the battery and make sure the water level is up to the ring just below the cap. Many new batteries are "closed cell" which means water cannot be added. Adding water will never, by itself, charge a battery and start an engine. It will allow the battery to regain its charge once the engine starts and the alternator operates. Maintain water level to ensure the health of your batteries.

The only "quick fix" at the batteries is the discovery and tightening of a loose cable. Gently twist the cables on the battery posts. A cable loose enough to reduce the power flow would move easily. Be careful not to loosen the post itself or you will create a more serious problem. Remove a loose cable and clean the contact area inside the terminal with sand paper or a wire brush. Adjust by tightening the nut on the cable end. Again, use force sparingly.

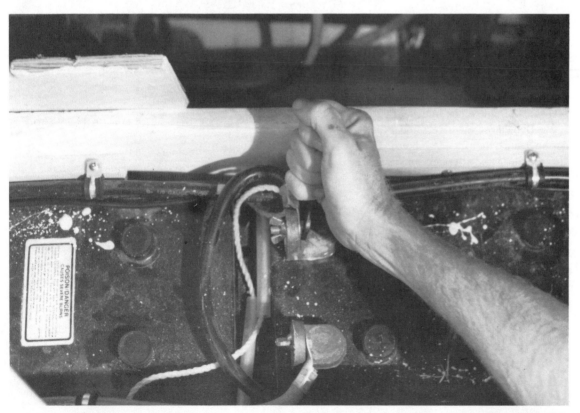

Loose battery terminals may cause partial or complete DC electrical system failure.

THE STARTER

Your previous inspection of the engine located the starter motor. It receives power from the solenoid switch which is often mounted on the starter motor. Follow the heavy cable from the battery switch and you will find the solenoid and the nearby starter.

Once again, check the cable connection and tighten if necessary. Never allow the wrench to contact the engine or other grounded metal while tightening a positive battery cable. It will cause a potentially dangerous spark. Overall the starter is not a serviceable item in the field, but a few light taps on the starter and solenoid have been known to free rust or corrosion inside the motor and allow the starter to operate.

(A) starter motor,
(B) solenoid

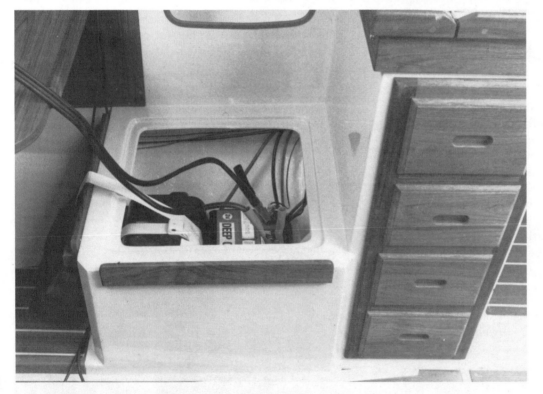

JUMPING THE BATTERIES

Your best prospect for giving the electrical system enough of a boost to get home is to jump the batteries just as you would those in a car. It usually requires very long cables to reach from the batteries of one boat to those of another. Two sets of cables can be clipped together as long as red goes to red and black to black. Use insulation material, such as rubber or plastic, to keep the black terminals from touching the red terminals where the cables meet. Violent sparks could result and lead to an electrical short on either boat.

Select a battery on your boat. Turn the battery switch to the setting for that battery. Place the battery switch on the other boat to "All" and start the engine. Select either battery and attach the cables, red to positive and black to negative. Do the same on the chosen battery. Be sure the cable's jaws make good contact with the battery terminal to permit more energy to flow to the disabled battery. Follow starting procedures for your boat.

A jump started engine will not re-start without another jump start if the battery fails to accept a charge while the engine is running. Your goal after starting the engine should be to get the boat to a place where the cause of the problem can be determined and fixed.

ENGINE PROBLEMS

A myriad of complications could plague a diesel engine and render it inoperable. The following are a few of the most common. Refer to other texts from the bibliography for a detailed treatment of the subject.

FUEL BLOCKAGE

Your below deck inspection in Section II covered the fuel system's components. Clean fuel, free of water, must arrive at the injector pump before the engine can start and run smoothly. If the engine turns over but will not start, determine whether or not fuel is flowing to the injector pump.

Find the fitting for the injector pump fuel intake line. Loosen it from the injector pump. Operate the lift pump if it is so equipped. Otherwise, have a crew member turn the key on to activate an electric fuel pump or turn the engine over for the manual variety. Run the pump for a few seconds. Fuel should spurt freely out of the fuel line. Anything other than a minor torrent indicates blockage or restriction. Performing this check almost guarantees having to bleed air from the fuel system but an inoperable engine probably would need bleeding anyway.

Leave the fuel line disconnected if a blockage has been discovered. Turn off the fuel line petcock if the system has one. Begin with the filter closest to the fuel tank. If your fuel separator contains a filter, disassemble it and replace the element with a new one.

Fuel flows into the filter canister around the outside of the element. The fuel pump draws fuel out through the tube extending down the center of the element. As fuel passes through the element, filtering material catches and holds foreign particles. If no replacement is available, clean the element in a shallow container of diesel fuel by gently rubbing along the outside and rinsing. Keep the dirty fuel out of the tube. Blowing air through the tube might dislodge enough particulate to allow adequate fuel to flow. Do so only if you are prepared to live with the taste of diesel fuel.

Repeat the process of replacing or cleaning filter elements along the fuel line toward the engine. Blow out lines between filters. Try turning the engine over again. If the fuel at the injector pump has increased, the engine should run. If not, you may have blockage in the tank or a fuel pump problem. Repairing these problems probably exceeds your ability.

BLEEDING THE FUEL SYSTEM

Air may have entered the fuel injection system before or after you disconnected the fuel line. Air in the fuel system is the most common cause of diesel engine failure. Try starting the engine with the line re-attached. Sometimes resumption of the normal fuel supply makes bleeding unnecessary.

Bleed the system by following these steps.

1. **Locate the tubing running from the injector pump to the injectors.**

2. **Open the connection at the injector closest to the injector pump.** Do not take the fitting completely off. Turn it counter clockwise a few turns, then go to step 3. If fuel does not flow loosen it further, a turn at a time, until it does.

3. **Crank the engine with the starter until fuel flows smoothly out of the fitting and no more bubbles can be seen or heard.**

4. **Tighten the fitting.**

5. **Repeat the process for each injector, working away from the injector pump, until the last injector has been bled.**

Be prepared for the engine to start while you crank the engine. As you hover over the injectors, make sure all loose clothing and tools are secure and away from moving engine parts.

Some diesel engines are very temperamental. Repeat the bleeding process two or three times before deciding to call a mechanic.

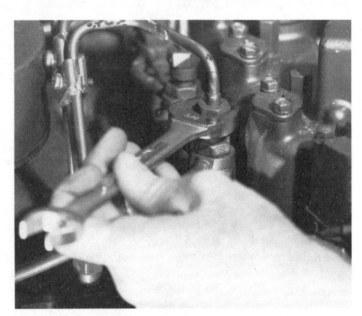

Turn coupling nut counter-clockwise to bleed injectors.

SPARE PARTS & SUPPLIES

Some problems described in this section can be put quickly behind you if the proper replacement parts are readily available. Boat owners have greater control over the parts inventory than sailors who charter. Charterers may decide to carry some parts in their gear bags. Here is a list of some of the things thatcould help in an emergency.

Electrical
Light bulbs
Fuses
Insulated wire (various sizes)
DC connectors
Insulated tape
Distilled water for batteries
Spare batteries for safety gear

Plumbing
Hose clamps (various sizes)
Extra tubing
Tubing repair material
Holding tank chemicals
Wood plugs

Mechanical
Spare filter elements
Impellors
Belts

Hoses
Oil
Engine coolant
Transmission fluid

Tools
4 1n screwdriver
Vice grips
Adjustable open end wrench
Rigging knife w/shackler
Electrical Wiresnips

Rigging
Spare shackles, lines,
cotter pins, split rings
Rip stop
Rigger's palm
 waxed twine
Heavy duty needles
20' - 30' of 1/8" nylon cord

CONCLUSION

By conquering the material in *Cruising Fundamentals* you have arrived at a crossroads visited by many other people who achieve their education and training aspirations. The time has come to put your lessons into practice and raise yourself to a higher sailing standard. Your goals need not know any bounds. Advanced Coastal Cruising, Celestial Navigation, Offshore Passagemaking or circumnavigation all lie within your grasp. *Cruising Fundamentals* supplies one important stepping stone for your advancement through a progressive sailing education. Regardless of your future in sailing or sailing education, you should feel lucky that your curiosity has guided you to a reliable learning resource and proud that you acquired the knowledge its pages had to offer.

Appendix A

ASA Bareboat Chartering Checklist

Individuals seeking ASA certification to the Bareboat Chartering (Intermediate Coastal Cruising) Standard will be tested on the Sailing Knowledge and Sailing Skills presented in this book. A detailed list of topics is contained in the ASA Cruising Log Book.

The checklist below has been re-printed from the ASA Bareboat Chartering exam. Instructors use this list to record an individual's ability to perform the skills necessary to receive the certification.

CHECK OUTS
- ❏ Engine Daily Check
- ❏ Engine Weekly Check
- ❏ First Aid Kit
- ❏ Tool Kit
- ❏ Stove
- ❏ Electronics
- ❏ Hull
- ❏ Rigging
- ❏ Sails

SAILING EFFICIENCY
- ❏ All Points of Sail
- ❏ Tacking
- ❏ Jibing
- ❏ Sailing To Weather
- ❏ Maneuvering Under Power
- ❏ Docking
- ❏ Turning (confined spaces)
- ❏ Stop Within 4 feet of a Marker
- ❏ Bow-to or Stern-to Docking with Anchor

COLLISION REGULATIONS
- ❏ As Opportunities Arise

VHF
- ❏ Sending and Receiving Calls

OPERATING THE STOVE
- ❏ Proper Safety Checks
- ❏ Proper Lighting Techniques
- ❏ Proper Extinguishing Techniques

TOWING THE DINGHY
- ❏ Safety and Efficiency Techniques

SOUNDINGS
- ❏ Electronic and Manual Depth Checks
- ❏ Sail a Compass Course
- ❏ To and From Destinations

MAN OVERBOARD
- ❏ Two Return Methods
- ❏ Two Recovery Methods

NAVIGATION
- ❏ Lay a Course Line
- ❏ Determine ETA
- ❏ Identify Landmarks
- ❏ Fix Using Bearings
- ❏ Depth Using Chart
- ❏ Piloting into an Unfamiliar Harbor
- ❏ Use Chart and Natural Surroundings

ROPE WORK
- ❏ Rolling Hitch
- ❏ Truckers Hitch (cinch knot)
- ❏ Bowline

ANCHORING
- ❏ One Anchor
- ❏ Two Anchors
- ❏ Bow and Stern

Appendix B

INDEX

Appendix C
PRACTICE QUESTIONS ANSWERS

SECTION I

1. Aft
2. Toe rail
3. Stem fitting
4. Deck fillers
5. Wheel brake
6. True
7. False
8. False
9. True
10. False

SECTION II

1. Through-hulls
2. Transducers
3. Sump pump
4. Three, Macerator
5. Compressed natural gas (CNG), Liquified petroleum gas (LPG or propane)
6. Quart, gallon
7. VHF
8. Raw water strainer
9. Fuel separator
10. Range
11. False
12. True
13. False
14. False
15. True
16. True

SECTION III

1. Compressed natural gas (CNG)
2. Water
3. Solenoid switch
4. Through hull
5. Land or horizon
6. Sea
7. Radiation
8. One, four to six
9. The host country
10. Skipper
11. False
12. True
13. True
14. True
15. False

SECTION IV

1. 360
2. Customs
3. Rafted
4. Capsize
5. Personal Flotation Device (PFD)
6. Four
7. Cooling water
8. False
9. True
10. False
11. True
12. False

Advection fog — Can occur any time warm, moist air blows over a surface cool enough to drop its temperature below the dew point.

Ammeter — An instrument for measuring electrical current in amperes.

Apparent wind — The wind strength and direction measured from the deck of a boat. The boat's speed and direction alter the affect of the true wind.

Azimuth circle — A ring designed to fit snugly over a compass and provided with means for observing compass bearings and azimuths.

Backwinding — Directing wind force onto the back or low pressure side of a sail.

Bearings — The direction from one object to another measured in either true or magnetic degrees.

Binnacle — A stand or pedestal, near the helm, where the ship's compass is mounted.

Bolt Rope — A line sewn into the luff or foot of a sail which allows the sail to be secured in a groove along a spar.

Bulkhead — A vertical partition in a hull that strengthens and/or separates.

Chocks — Fairlead used to direct anchor or mooring lines.

Cunningham — Block and tackle system used to exert tension on the luff of a sail.

Dead Reckoning — The process of plotting a position based on advancing from a known position using speed and time.

Deviation — Differences between a compass' reading and an actual magnetic direction caused by magnetic forces in the vicinity of the compass.

Fairlead — A fitting used to guide a line in a particular direction.

Fairway — A major channel or portion of a major channel used for navigation.

Flake — (1) To lay a line out in coils so that it can run without fouling. (2) Folding a sail in layers on a spar.

Forecastle — A cabin located forward of the main mast and used for housing crew members on traditional sailing ships.

Gate valve — A fitting with a faucet-like handle used to restrict the flow of water in a line.

GPS — Global Positioning System. A satellite based navigation system capable of fixing a position with great accuracy.

Hawser — A line or cable used for towing.

Headfoil — A metal extrusion fitted on a forestay and used to secure the luff of a sail by holding its bolt rope in place.

Hypothermia — A lowering of the body's core temperature resulting in loss of motor control, unconsciousness and death.

Inland Rules — Navigation rules applying to vessels inside designated demarcation lines.

International America's Cup Class — Sailing yachts, approximately 75 feet long, designed for America's Cup competition beginning in 1992.

International Date Line — A line of longitude positioned approximately 180° opposite Greenwich, England. The sun's passage directly above this line causes an advancement of the date.

International Rules — Navigation rules applying to vessels outside designated demarcation lines.

Jack lines — Lines running along the deck between the bow and stern used to attach a tether from a safety harness.

Latitude — Calibrating lines running east and west parallel to the equator measuring distance north and south from 0° to 90°.

Lazarette — Compartment in the stern of a boat used for storage.

Lead line — Calibrated line and weight lowered from the deck of a boat to determine water depth.

Lombard shot — A cannon ball used in Columbus' time.

Longitude — Great circle lines running north and south pointing to true north measuring distance east and west 180° from the prime meridian (Greenwich, England)

Lubber line — A line on the compass aligned with the center line of the boat that indicates the boat's heading on the compass.

Marlin spike — Pointed tool used for line work especially for prying tight knots apart.

Masthead — Top of the mast.

Mizzen — A sail located on a smaller, aft-mounted mast on a ketch or yawl.

Navigation Rules — The complete set of published rules governing navigation.

NOAA — National Oceanographic and Atmospheric Administration. A government agency whose duties include distribution of nautical charts and weather broadcasts.

Outhaul — A control line that exerts force along the foot of a sail pulling the clew away from the tack.

Pad eye — A loop-shaped fitting used to secure a line to some part of the boat.

Phonetic alphabet — A universally accepted group of words corresponding to the letters of the alphabet and used in radio transmissions to avoid confusing similar sounding letters.

Preventer — A line, often the boom vang, used to hold the boom in place while reaching or running, preventing an uncontrolled boom swing during an accidental jibe.

Prop walk — Sideward force created by a spinning propellor.

Prow — The bow and forward part of the vessel above the waterline.

Radiation fog — Fog over land caused by condensation of vapor in the air above cooler ground.

Range — The distance a boat can travel using the fuel it can store.

Running rigging — Adjustable sail controls

Running spring line — Spring line which is adjusted from onboard the boat and used to position it on the way out of a slip or mooring.

Salvage — Saving or recovering a vessel or its cargo.

Sea breezes — Wind drawn ashore by rising thermal air currents caused by the heating of land.

Sea room — Distance away from shore, a sea wall or other obstruction.

Seacock — A valve, operated by a movable handle that restricts the flow of water in a line.

Separator — Component in a diesel fuel system used to separate water from fuel.

Sheave — The grooved part of a block through which a line runs.

Shipping lanes — Portions of open water reserved for commercial shipping and designated as such on a chart.

Strainer — Filtering device used to remove solid debris from cooling water.

Strut — Metal fitting that supports and aligns the aft portion of a propellor shaft.

Stuffing box — A fitting that seals and lubricates the propellor shaft in the area where it protrudes through the hull.

Subordinate station — A location near a reference station whose daily tidal information is recorded in the tide tables.

Telltales — Yarn or other lightweight material attached to parts of the boat or sails and used to determine the wind direction.

Tether — A line attached between a person's safety harness and a secure part of the boat.

Tidal range — The difference in depth between high and low tide.

Track — The course a boat travels over the ground.

Traffic separation zone — An area between opposite flowing shipping lanes restricted to most navigation.

Trip line — A line attached to the crown of an anchor and used to free it in the event it becomes fouled.

Turnbuckles — Threaded adjusters used to tension stays and shrouds.

Turning blocks — Horizontally mounted blocks used to re-direct a line on deck.

Underway — A vessel is underway when it is not affixed to land, moored or anchored.

Variation — The difference between true and magnetic north found in the compass rose expressed in degrees and minutes.

Weather helm — The tendency of a sailboat to turn into the wind. The rudder must be held at an angle to keep the boat from rounding-up.

Whisker pole — A pole, often adjustable in length, used to hold the clew of a jib away from the mast.

Y valve — Liquid flows into the valve and flows out through one of two tubes which are selected by changing the angle of a lever.

Yarn — A tall tale.

Appendix E
CHECKLISTS

PRE-SAIL CHECKLIST

- ❏ Open and ventilate cabin
- ❏ Turn battery switch to "both" or "all"
- ❏ Test Batteries if meter is equipped
- ❏ Turn on VHF, monitor weather channel, perform radio check
- ❏ Locate and inspect safety gear
- ❏ Check bilge water level, pump dry
- ❏ Locate through hulls, open appropriate valves
- ❏ Check other through hulls for water tight integrity
- ❏ Test head and check waste routing
- ❏ Check battery, oil, transmission and coolant levels
- ❏ Check belt tension and inspect hoses
- ❏ Locate charts for sailing area
- ❏ Activate and inspect all navigation lights
- ❏ Disconnect shore power and properly stow cable
- ❏ Remove sail cover and other covers
- ❏ Attach jib (non-furling) and run sheets
- ❏ Attach halyards and check for fouling
- ❏ Check fuel level
- ❏ Open fuel shut-off

- ❏ Top off water tank(s)
- ❏ Check function of stove and fuel level
- ❏ Stow all gear
- ❏ Inspect rigging
- ❏ Inspect ground tackle
- ❏ File float plan

DAILY CHECK LIST

- ❏ Check bilge level, pump dry
- ❏ Check water levels
- ❏ Check holding tank and arrange pumping if necessary
- ❏ Check fuel level
- ❏ Check oil level
- ❏ Check coolant level
- ❏ Monitor weather channel, radio check
- ❏ Start engine, check water discharge and gauges

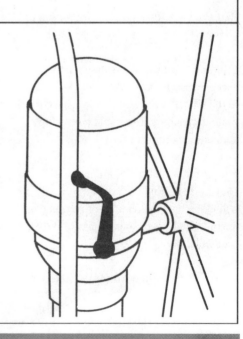

WEEKLY CHECKLIST

Perform daily checklist plus:

❏ Check transmission fluid level

❏ Inspect belts and hoses

❏ Inspect rigging

❏ Inspect ground tackle

❏ Check long term weather forecast

❏ Activate and inspect all lights

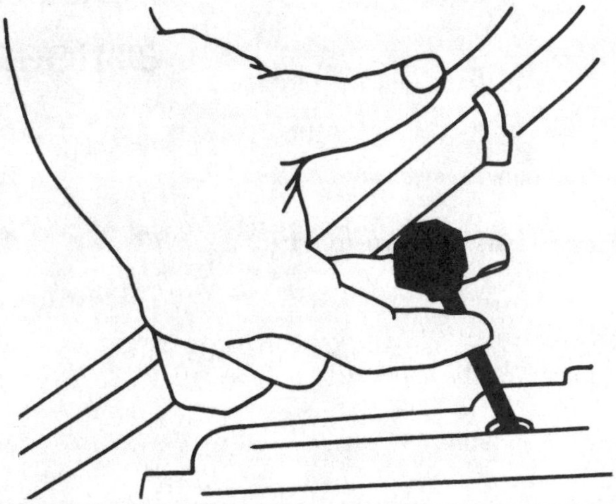

DAILY POST-SAIL CHECKLIST

❏ Monitor anchor swing radius of early and late arrivals

❏ Check that battery setting is on "1" or "2"

❏ Secure halyards

❏ Cover main sail

❏ Fold and stow jib (non-furling)

❏ Secure and coil all lines

❏ Rig chafing gear on anchor rode

❏ Secure dinghy and outboard

❏ Set an anchor watch

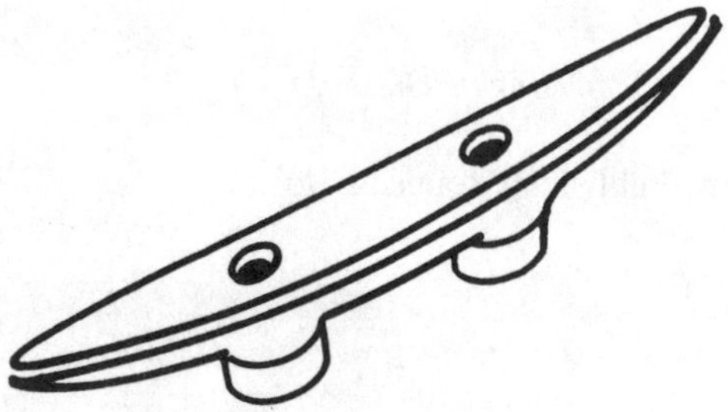

SECURING THE SAILBOAT

❏ Secure all dock lines

❏ Secure halyards

❏ Fold and cover mainsail

❏ Fold and stow jib (non-furling)

❏ Secure and coil all lines

❏ Replace other covers

❏ Attach shore power

❏ Close through hulls

❏ Secure and stow winch handles, PFDs, jib sheets etc.

❏ Close hatches

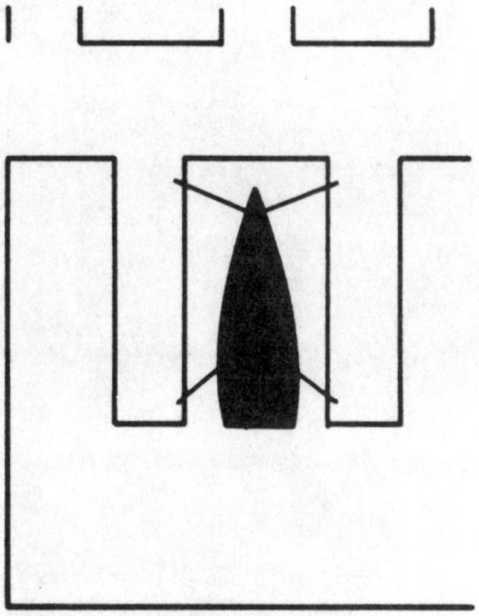

❏ Turn battery switch "off"

❏ Secure all fenders, spring and dock lines

Appendix F
BIBLIOGRAPHY

Chapman, C. F. Piloting, *Seamanship and Small Boat Handling*. 57th ed. Hearst Publications, New York, 1987.

Rousmaniere, John. *The Annapolis Book of Seamanship.* Simon & Shuster, New York, 1983.

Fagan, Brian. *Chartering Fundamentals.* The American Sailing Association, Los Angeles, CA, 1987.

Thiel, Richard. *Keep Your Marine Diesel Running,* International Marine Publishing, Camden, ME 1991.

Jobson, Gary. *Sailing Fundamentals.* American Sailing Association, Los Angeles, CA 1987

Graves, Fredrick. *The Big Book of Marine Electronics.* Seven Seas Press, Newport, RI 1985

Stapleton, Ted. *Emergencies at Sea.* Simon & Shuster, New York, NY

Edwards, Fred. *Sailing as a Second Lanaguage.* International Marine Publishing, Camden, ME

NOTES

Team Members Receive Special Preference

To our members the ASA means more than certification and educational excellence. It's smart business! When you join the ASA, you become a member of America's strongest and fastest growing team. Team members enjoy a number of important benefits.

HAVE CARD WILL TRAVEL
Rental and Charter Discounts

Nearly 200 locations across the country honor the ASA membership card and offer rental and charter discounts on hundred of different sailboats. In addition, some ASA schools extend discount prices to classes and other club activities. Whether you just want to unwind for an afternoon during a business trip or take the family on a cruisingvacation, your ASA membership card makes things happen. Discounts on car rentals and accommodations get you to your destination for less Go ahead. Explore!

SLEEP CHEAP!

Quest allows you to stay at over 1,000 hotels nationwide at a 50% discount. Just show your membership card and you will automatically receive a 50% discount on your stay at participating hotels. ASA team members are eligible for Quest membership at an incredibly low price. We guarantee you save more than the membership price your first night's stay.

ASA Gold Mastercard

The cardoffers one hour credit line increases, lost baggage protection, travel accident insurance, car rental collision damage insurance and much more. Competitive interest rates and no annual fee the first year make this one of the best cards available.

AMERICAN SAILING
The Journal of the American Sailing Association

Each issue of American Sailing brings you features on exciting traditional and contemporary sailing topics, navigation and seamanship articles, nautical book and video reviews, Sea Stories and more. In addition the ASA journal keeps you up-to-date on the latest in ASA activities and new ways to enjoy the sport.

Team members can shop for the gear and equipment they need at great savings. Most items bear the ASA *Sailing Team* insignia. Sailors worldwide will recognize one another by the distinctive logo. Equip yourself and your family with quality gear and equipment from some of the world's leading manufacturers.

In addition, receive discounts coupons for goods and services from these companies:

Sail Magazine   The Moorings Worldwide Charters
Bennett Marine Video   International Marine Publishing
K-Swiss nautical footwear   National and International Travel
The ASA constantly adds the highest quality member benefits available.

Your Membership Fee Helps Sailing Itself

Your membership in the ASA doesn't just benefit you; it benefits sailing nationwide. The ASA is a highly active representative to the National Boating Federation, the International Sailing Schools Association and the National Association of Boating Law Administrators. ASA strongly opposes restrictive boating legislation and works overtime to encourage fresh thinking to make the sport of sailing safer and more enjoyable.

Helping To Keep Our Waters Clean

As a concerned sailor you can be proud knowing that a portion of your ASA membership dues goes toward helping to clean up our oceans and to keep them clean. We select environmental groups that are dedicated to keeping our waterways free of trash that is so harmful to our marine life.

Join Today

Join thousands of other discriminating sailors who need to stay well equipped, well informed and wish to exercise some control over the sport and lifestyle they love. Don't wait - the team needs you!

Name_____

Street Address_____

City_____ State_____ Zip_____

Daytime Phone_____

☐ Check of M. O. ☐ Mastercard ☐ Visa ☐ Amex

Card #_____ Exp._____

Signature_____

☐ $25 one-year individual
☐ $40 two-year individual
☐ $15 additional family member, per year
☐ $50 one-year family (list additional members)
☐ $85 two-year (list additional members)
☐ $250 individual lifetime membership
☐ $500 family lifetime membership (list additional members)

American Sailing Association
13922 Marquesas Way • Marina del Rey, CA 90292 • Phone (310) 822-7171 • Fax (310) 822-4741